THE AUSTRALIAN
Women's Weekly
Vegan
in 30
minutes

Published in 2019 by Bauer Media Books, Australia.
Bauer Media Books is a division of Bauer Media Pty Ltd.

Bauer Media Group

Chief Executive Officer
Brendon Hill

Chief Financial Officer
Andrew Stedwell

Bauer Media Books

Publisher
Sally Eagle

Editorial & Food Director
Sophia Young

Creative Director
Hannah Blackmore

Managing Editor
Stephanie Kistner

Senior Designer
Alexandra Cook

Editor
Amanda Lees

Food Editors
Sophia Young, Georgia Moore

Operations Manager
David Scotto

Cover Photographer
James Moffatt

Cover Stylist
Oliva Blackmore

Cover Photochef
Vikki Moursellas

Printed in China
by 1010 Printing International.

A catalogue record for this book
is available from the National
Library of Australia.
ISBN 978-1-92569-558-8

© Bauer Media Pty Limited 2019
Abn 18 053 273 546

Published by Bauer Media Books,
A Division Of Bauer Media Pty Ltd,
54 Park St, Sydney; Gpo Box 4088,
Sydney, Nsw 2001, Australia
Ph +61 2 8116 9334;
Fax +61 2 9126 3702
www.awwcookbooks.com.au

International Rights Manager
Simone Aquilina
saquilina@bauer-media.com.au
Ph +61 2 8268 6278

Order books
Phone 136 116 (Within Australia)

Or order online at
www.awwcookbooks.com.au

Send recipe enquiries to
recipeenquiries@bauer-media.com.au

Trusted brands used in our test kitchen

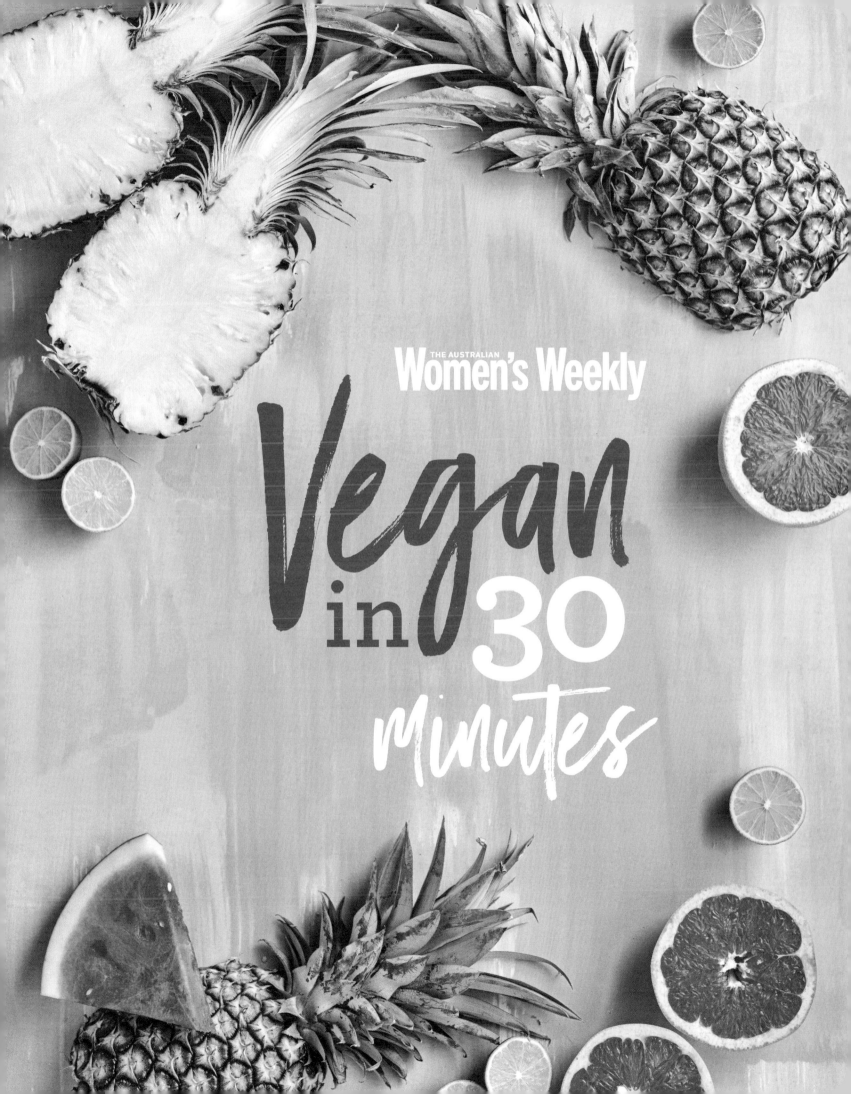

THE AUSTRALIAN
Women's Weekly

Vegan
in 30
minutes

Contents

6 Vegan living

12 Breakfast

48 Light lunches

108 Dinners

176 Snacks & sweets

232 Glossary

236 Conversion chart

237 Index

Vegan living

Whether you are already vegan or simply vegan-curious, interest in exploring the incredible range of plant-based foods has never been as popular as it is now.

What is a vegan diet?

A vegan diet is entirely plant-based, excluding all animal products. Not only are meat, seafood, eggs and dairy products off the menu, but also honey and gelatine. Whether it's for animal welfare, ecological or health reasons, veganism is becoming a more mainstream choice.

Veganism has often been characterised as restrictive, difficult and just plain hard work. Instead of focusing on what vegans don't eat, let's look at the abundance of ingredients vegans can enjoy:

Legumes

Includes dried and canned lentils, chickpeas, cannellini beans, kidney beans, borlotti beans, black-eye beans and green and yellow split peas.

Grains and grain substitutes/ pseudo-grains

Includes amaranth, barley, buckwheat, freekeh, oats, rice, farro, millet, polenta, quinoa, and wheat-based products such as flours, couscous and burghul.

Nuts and seeds

Almonds, cashews, peanuts, pecans, pistachios, macadamias, walnuts, sunflower seeds, pepitas, linseeds, chia seeds and sesame seeds, as well as unhulled and hulled tahini.

Soy products

Such as tofu, tempeh and other soy products, including miso and 'cheeses'.

Alternative milks

There is a wide range of milks now available, including soy milk, rice milk, almond milk, coconut milk and oat milk.

Sea vegetables

Includes nori, kombu, wakame and spirulina.

Herbs and spices

Keep a ready supply of spices such as cardamom, cinnamon, cloves, coriander, cumin, fennel seeds, garam masala, garlic powder, ginger, mustard seeds and powder, nutmeg, onion powder, paprika and turmeric. Fresh herbs, such as basil, coriander, dill, flat-leaf parsley, mint, oregano, rosemary and thyme add flavour and freshness.

Condiments

Including soy sauce, tamari, miso, vinegars, mustards and nutritional yeast flakes.

Your nutritional needs

When planning vegan meals, especially when starting out, the most frequently asked questions are about how to incorporate all the necessary nutrients into your diet. To help avoid potential deficiencies, here are the most common nutrients that cause concern and suggestions for vegan sources to meet your dietary needs:

Calcium

In place of dairy products, use nuts, seeds, leafy green vegetables, legumes, and soy products, especially those that are fortified with calcium.

Iodine

Include sea vegetables, such as nori, kombu or wakame and small amounts of iodised salt. Check with your doctor before taking supplements if you have a thyroid issue.

Iron

Eat nuts, lentils, oats, dried fruit, dark leafy green vegetables and soy products. Eating these in tandem with fresh vitamin C-rich food aids the body to better absorb the iron.

Vitamin C

Include tomatoes, red capsicum, broccoli, citrus fruit and berries in your diet.

Omega-3 fatty acids

Include linseeds, chia seeds, pepitas, seaweed, spirulina and walnuts.

Protein

Eat legumes, whole grains, quinoa, nuts, seeds and soy products, especially tofu and tempeh.

Vitamin B12

As this is only found in meat, incorporate foods fortified with vitamin B12, such as some cereals, plant-based milks and soy products. A supplement can be taken for healthy blood cells.

Zinc

Add whole grains, nuts, pepitas, wheatgerm and soy products, especially tofu and tempeh to your diet.

Your day on a plate

Active person

It is important if you fall into this category, especially if you are female and pre-menopausal, to ensure that you avoid restrictive food eating patterns, or you risk an inadequate dietary intake for optimum health. For the active vegan, incorporate energy dense foods such as nuts, tofu, tempeh and other quality protein at every meal. Since vegetable proteins don't include all the necessary amino acids required, it is necessary to combine a variety of proteins throughout the day. Also since plant-based proteins are not as easily digested as meat derived ones, it is advised that vegans consume 10% more. If you are vegan and super active it is especially important to target iron-rich foods and monitor your iron stores. To ensure sufficient calcium intake look for calcium-rich vegan food, such as almonds, leafy greens and broccoli.

Moderately active person

The nutritional requirements of a moderately active person are very similar to that of an active person. The main difference between the two is that your overall kilojoule requirements will be less. Also, your carb requirements may be reduced. As with a vegan diet in general, balance and eating widely from all plant-based foods are key to ensure that you are capturing vital nutrients and are not missing out on certain nutritional requirements that can be harder to meet in a vegan diet. There are many vegan foods that are not necessarily healthy. In fact many manufactured vegan substitutes can be laden with not so useful bulking agents that can add unnecessarily to your kilojoule quota. Also, just because sweet treats are vegan doesn't afford them health-food status.

Vegan pantry

Across each day look to fill your plate with a wide array of colourful vegetables, fruits, wholegrains, legumes, nuts and seeds, while also including healthy fats, like avocado and extra virgin olive oil for a balanced diet.

Probiotics

These include micro-organisms found in lactic acid bacteria, yeast and moulds. They work in tandem with prebiotics, non-digestible food fibres to support good gut health. Vegan sources include: sauerkraut (1), kimchi, miso, tempeh and kombucha. Prebiotic-rich foods include: oats, legumes, green vegetables and bananas.

Legumes

Essential in the vegan diet, legumes provide high protein, slow-release carbs and are a useful source of the B-group vitamins, especially folate. They also contain iron, magnesium, calcium and zinc. From tiny quick-cooking lentils to larger beans, like chickpeas (2), and even peanuts, which are technically a legume, all are valuable.

Nutritional powders

These are great flavour boosters with powerful antioxidants. Matcha powder (3), dried green tea, works in both sweet and savoury dishes (see our Matcha mint raw slice, page 203). Acai powder, from an Amazon wild berry is another to try in smoothies or raw puddings. Raw cacao, with a slightly bitter taste retains more of its nutrients than regular cocoa.

Chia seeds (4)

A particularly rich source of omega-3 fatty acids, which is more commonly found in fish and meat, and soluble fibre. As with all seeds they are nutritionally dense, providing protein, a variety of vitamins, minerals and trace elements. And like sesame seeds, chia seeds are high in calcium. Also add pepitas, linseeds and sunflower seeds to your pantry.

Soy products

Tempeh, tofu and soy (5) all provide vegans with a high-quality source of protein, complete with essential amino acids. They are also low in unsaturated fats (the exception is tofu puffs) and contain

B vitamins. However, there is a question mark around high consumption of soy products and its potential to harm male fertility.

Nutritional yeast flakes (6)

A seasoning used to provide a moreish cheese-like umami taste. To get the most bang for your buck, buy a brand that is fortified with B12, a vitamin required for the development of healthy blood cells and the prevention of anaemia, which is only available from fortified foods or via a supplement on a vegan diet.

Nuts

These add a wide spectrum of nutrients to a vegan diet. They provide a combination of good healthy monounsaturated and polyunsaturated fats, moderate amounts of protein and dietary fibre. Some can be singled out for unique attributes: almonds (7) for protein, calcium and magnesium; cashews for iron and walnuts for plant omega-3 fatty acids.

Grains

Choose those that are whole and unrefined as they have the most nutritional benefits and help with satiety. The cooking properties of quinoa (8) mean that although it is a seed it is referred to as a pseudo-grain. It is one of a few plant-based foods that contain all essential amino acids, making it a complete protein. And also because it's not technically a grain, it's completely gluten-free.

Sea vegetables

Nori (9), wakami, kelp and kombu are rich with nutrients and are a source of essential vitamins and minerals. In particular they are high in iodine, needed for healthy thyroid function, which in turn aids your metabolism. Too much iodine can be just as damaging as too little, so as with most foods, eat broadly and avoid supplements without consulting your doctor.

Helpful links

Animals Australia
www.animalsaustralia.org

Australia's leading animal protection organisation, spearheading important investigations and campaigns.

Choose Cruelty Free (CCF)
www.choosecrueltyfree.org.au

This independent, not-for-profit organisation produces The Choose Cruelty Free List, a booklet listing companies and brand names that operate under a cruelty-free ethic to help consumers make well informed choices.

People for the Ethical Treatment of Animals (PETA)
www.peta.org.au

The largest global organisation in the world for animal protection, whose mission statement is – 'animals are not ours to eat, wear, experiment on, use for entertainment, or abuse in any other way.' The local website includes useful links to food, fashion and vegan beauty retailers, as well as campaigns.

The Cruelty Free Shop
www.crueltyfreeshop.com.au

With retail stores in four Australian states and territories, plus an online shop with over 3,500 vegan items.

Vegan Australia
www.veganaustralia.org.au

This website provides a wide range of services to new and existing vegans from event listings, news, vegan nutrition to details on campaigns.

Barnivore
www.barnivore.com

An online directory of vegan and vegetarian beer, wine, and liquor.

Meal prep like a boss

Planning and meal prep are great to help you achive healthy and stress-free vegan eating, as there's no decision making required at meal times, you just need to sit down and eat. A degree of planning with shopping and prepping will assist in keeping you on track, ensuring you always have a well-stocked vegan kitchen.

Meal planning

Dedicate one day a week to preparing a weekly menu and shopping list. This way you are not pressed to think of what to cook after a busy tiring day. Sunday is often a good day for full-time workers to jump into the kitchen and make a head start on the upcoming week's cooking.

Bulk shop dry goods weekly

Save time by doing a regular bulk shop of all your dry ingredients, as well as longer lasting vegetables, so all you need to shop for are perishables.

Organise the pantry

A clean organised pantry helps you find items quickly. Transfer opened items to clear labelled and dated glass storage containers. Aim to always have a good selection of staples, such as canned beans, tomatoes and grains.

Cook double

Look for recipes that can be doubled and eaten over multiple nights. Not all food will last all week in the fridge so aim to also use the freezer for storage.

Find ingredient overlaps

When you are creating your weekly menu look for recipes that share ingredients like rice, quinoa or leafy greens so that you can cook them ahead.

Containers

Purchase good quality BPA-free plastic or glass containers for food storage. Use plastic for the freezer as glass containers can expand and crack. And don't forget to clearly label your containers.

Equipment

Take advantage of a mandoline, V-slicer, food processor or Thermomix, if you have one, to assist with the prep.

Decoding labels

While at first it may seem that avoiding animal products is fraught, there are many websites to help you and encouragingly, savvy food companies recognise that a vegan-lifestyle is an important part of their market share and are assisting with labelling their products.

In order to make an informed choice around the consumption of animal-based products it is necessary to know the names of certain animal-based ingredients that are hidden away in everyday food stuffs. The good thing to know is the more you eat minimally processed foods, the less likely you are to encounter them.

Hidden dairy

Vegans avoid dairy and therefore animal rennet, a coagulate commonly used in cheese making. Other dairy-based ingredients to watch out for are: casein, whey, lactalbumin, lactose, lactulose, nougat candy and ghee (derived from butter) and the Indian dairy-based cheese paneer. Lactic acid is used in beer, sauerkraut, pickles and products that use bacterial fermentation.

Hidden seafood products

Anchovies are hidden away in caesar dressings and many brands of worcestershire sauce, while fish sauce is a common ingredient in Thai curry pastes and takeaways. Isinglass, a fish-based gelatine-like product can turn up in alcoholic drinks and jelly desserts.

Hidden meat products

Gelatine is in marshmallows, gummy-style confectionery and is a common coating for pills. Sugar can be refined through bone char, though this is not the case with Australian produced sugar. Tallow, animal shortening, pops up in refried beans, tortillas and ready-made pastries.

Hidden egg products

Egg yolk is common in dried ribbon pasta. Albumin, derived from egg whites may be used as a fining agent and may not be declared on wines and liqueurs labels. Check websites for vegan-friendly brands.

Whilst there is no official vegan logo, Vegan Australia is attempting to make it easier for all those choosing vegan.

Breakfast

serves 2

Scrambled tofu bagel

15 mins

food swaps

To add a smoky flavour to the scrambled tofu use smoked tofu, available from combined greengrocer delis and delis. You could also use other spicy, flavoured hummus, like jalapeño or harissa hummus. Top with other leafy greens such as rocket and watercress.

250g (8oz) firm tofu
2 teaspoons nutritional yeast flakes (optional) (see tip)
½ teaspoon ground turmeric
½ teaspoon cumin seeds
¼ teaspoon smoked paprika
2 tablespoons extra virgin olive oil
4 green onions (scallions), sliced thinly
1 clove garlic, crushed
1 tablespoon coarsely chopped fresh flat-leaf parsley
1 tablespoon lemon juice
4 bagels (169g), split, toasted
⅓ cup (90g) chipotle hummus (see food swaps)
2 medium tomatoes (300g), sliced
50g (1½oz) baby spinach leaves
½ cup snow pea tendrils (optional)

1 Pat tofu dry with paper towel to remove excess moisture. Crumble tofu into a bowl, using your hands.

2 Combine nutritional yeast, turmeric, cumin seeds, paprika and 1 tablespoon water in a small bowl; season with salt and pepper.

3 Heat oil in a medium frying pan over medium-high heat; cook green onion and garlic for 1 minute or until softened. Add crumbled tofu; cook, stirring, for 4 minutes or until tofu starts to brown a little. Add the spice mixture; cook, stirring, for 1 minute or until tofu is completely coated. Stir in parsley and juice until combined.

4 Spread toasted bagel halves with hummus; top bases with tomato, scrambled tofu, spinach leaves and snow pea tendrils.

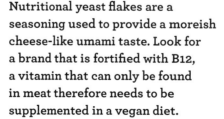

TIP

Nutritional yeast flakes are a seasoning used to provide a moreish cheese-like umami taste. Look for a brand that is fortified with B12, a vitamin that can only be found in meat therefore needs to be supplemented in a vegan diet.

serves 2

Avo toast with smoky crisp chickpeas

 15 mins

 vegan hacks

If you have leftover canned chickpeas, reserve them for the Sweet potatoes with chickpea tabbouleh, page 117.

1 cup (190g) drained canned chickpeas (garbanzo beans), rinsed
2 tablespoons extra virgin olive oil
½ teaspoon sea salt flakes
½ teaspoon smoked paprika
½ teaspoon ground cumin
4 slices wholegrain sourdough bread (200g), toasted
1 large avocado (320g), mashed
⅓ cup soft herbs (see tip)
2 tablespoons sriracha
lime wedges, to serve

1 Pat chickpeas dry with paper towel. Heat oil in a large frying pan over high heat; cook chickpeas and salt, stirring occasionally, for 5 minutes. Add the paprika and cumin; cook, stirring, for a further 30 seconds.

2 Spread toasted sourdough with mashed avocado. Top with smoky chickpeas and soft herbs; drizzle with sriracha. Serve with lime wedges.

TIP
You can use any chopped soft-leaf herb such as fresh flat-leaf parsley, dill, coriander (cilantro) or mint to top your avocado toast.

Berry co-yo crunch bowl

serves 6

1 cup (160g) brazil nuts
½ cup (80g) almonds
⅓ cup (65g) pepitas (pumpkin seed kernels)
⅓ cup (50g) sunflower seeds
⅔ cup (30g) unsweetened flaked coconut
¼ cup (35g) cacao nibs
⅔ cup (110g) inca berries or sultanas
3 cups (840g) berry coconut yoghurt
fresh fruit and edible flowers, to serve (see serving ideas)

1 Preheat oven to 180°C/350°F.

2 Place brazil nuts and almonds on an oven tray; roast for 10 minutes or until browned lightly and fragrant. Chop nuts coarsely; place in a large bowl. Roast seeds on oven tray for 8 minutes or until browned lightly; add to bowl. Roast coconut on oven tray for 4 minutes or until browned lightly and fragrant. Add to bowl with cacao nibs and inca berries; stir to combine.

3 Serve crunch bowl mix in serving bowls with yoghurt. Top with fruit and edible flowers.

30 mins

vegan hacks

Serve the crunch bowl mix as a muesli, or sprinkle on top of yoghurt or fruit, scattered with edible flowers and vegan chocolate, if you like. It also doubles as a trail mix for an energy-rich snack on the go.

serving ideas

Serve crunch bowl topped with dragonfruit, honeydew, figs, kiwifruit, cherries, blueberries, strawberries, pomegranate seeds and raspberries. You can use any combination of seasonal fruits you prefer.

TIP Any combination of nuts and seeds can be used in this recipe. Inca berries are high in vitamins C, B and A and are available at some supermarkets and health food stores.

Warming quinoa porridge

serves 4

 15 mins

 food swaps

Try replacing apples with pears, blueberries with strawberries and hazelnuts with almonds for a new flavour.

1 litre (4 cups) soy milk or nut milk
3 granny smith apples (450g), grated coarsely
1 teaspoon vanilla extract
125g (4oz) blueberries
¾ cup (70g) quinoa flakes
¼ cup (50g) black chia seeds
⅓ cup (95g) unsweetened coconut or other vegan yoghurt
⅓ cup (45g) skinless roasted hazelnuts, chopped coarsely
⅓ cup (80ml) pure maple syrup

1 Place milk, apple and vanilla in a medium saucepan over low heat; cook for 5 minutes or until milk is almost boiling and apple is softened.

2 Lightly crush half the blueberries, add to the pan with quinoa flakes and chia seeds; cook, stirring, for 5 minutes or until thickened.

3 Serve porridge topped with yoghurt, hazelnuts and remaining blueberries. Drizzle with maple syrup.

5 mins

 food swaps

You can use any non-dairy milk.

 vegan hacks

LSA is a ground mixture of linseeds (L), sunflower seeds (S) and almonds (A). It is available from supermarkets and health food stores.

Soy, linseed & raspberry smoothie

1 large banana (230g), chopped
1 cup (150g) frozen raspberries
2 cups (500ml) soy milk
1 tablespoon tahini
1 tablespoon LSA (see vegan hacks)
1 tablespoon pure maple syrup

1 Blend ingredients in a high-powered blender until smooth.

2 Serve smoothie topped with fresh raspberries and toasted sesame seeds, if you like.

Smoothies

makes
1 litre

⏳ **10 mins**

🍽 **serving idea**

Serve with sliced pear and sprinkled with chia seeds.

Power green smoothie

1 small celery stalk (55g), chopped
2 cups (90g) chopped kale leaves
2 cups (500ml) chilled coconut water
1 small ripe pear (180g), cored, chopped
1 medium ripe banana (200g), sliced
½ medium ripe avocado (125g), sliced
1 tablespoon grated fresh ginger
1 tablespoon white chia seeds
1 cup ice cubes

1 Blend celery, kale and coconut water in a high-powered blender until smooth.

2 Add pear, banana, avocado, ginger, chia seeds and ice; blend until smooth and creamy.

TIP

Green smoothies have a basic formula which is 2 cups greens, 2 cups liquid and 2 cups fruit. Experiment with whatever fruit is in season.

Chia crêpes with banana & blueberries

1 tablespoon white chia seeds
¾ cup (110g) plain (all-purpose) flour
½ teaspoon ground cinnamon
2½ tablespoons coconut sugar
1 cup (250ml) almond milk
30g (1oz) coconut oil, melted
4 sugar bananas (520g), halved lengthways (see vegan hacks)
⅔ cup (190g) coconut or vegan yoghurt
2 tablespoons blueberries
2 teaspoons black sesame seeds

1 Combine chia seeds and ½ cup (125ml) boiling water in a small heatproof cup; stand 5 minutes.

2 Place the flour, cinnamon and 2 teaspoons of the coconut sugar in a medium bowl. Make a well in the centre; gradually whisk in combined almond milk and chia seed mixture until smooth.

3 Heat a 26cm (10½in) (top measurement) non-stick frying pan over a high heat. Lightly grease with some of the coconut oil. Pour ½ cup of the batter into the centre of the hot pan, tilting pan to coat the base in a thin layer; cook for 1 minute or until browned. Turn, cook on the other side until golden. Transfer to a plate; cover with foil to keep warm. Repeat with remaining batter, greasing with coconut oil, to make a total of 4 crêpes.

4 Reduce heat under pan to medium-high heat. Sprinkle remaining sugar on cut-side of the banana halves. Cook cut-side down in pan for 1 minute or until caramelised.

5 Divide crêpes between plates. Top with caramelised banana, yoghurt and blueberries; sprinkle with sesame seeds.

 25 mins

 vegan hacks

Sugar bananas, also known as finger bananas are smaller and sweeter than regular bananas. If unavailable use regular bananas, halved lengthways and crossways.

 TIP The hotter the pan the better the crêpes, however remove the pan from the heat for a few seconds between each crêpe so that they don't burn.

Spiced pecan french toast

**serves
4**

**25
mins**

**food
swaps**

Use almond meal instead of hazelnut meal and olive oil instead of vegan margarine.

1½ cups (375ml) coconut milk
2 teaspoons vanilla extract
½ cup (125ml) pure maple syrup
⅓ cup (35g) hazelnut meal
¼ teaspoon mixed spice
1 cup (120g) pecans, chopped finely
8 x 50g (1½oz) slices thick
   multigrain sourdough bread
40g (1½oz) vegan margarine
fresh or frozen berries and edible
   flowers, to serve (optional)

1 Whisk coconut milk, vanilla, 2 tablespoons of the syrup, the hazelnut meal and mixed spice in a shallow dish. Place pecans on a plate. Soak bread in coconut milk mixture, one at a time, for 1 minute each side. Press onto pecans.

2 Heat half the margarine in a large frying pan over low-medium heat; cook bread, in batches, for 2 minutes each side or until golden, adding remaining margarine halfway through cooking time.

3 Divide french toast among plates; drizzle with remaining maple syrup. Serve topped with berries and edible flowers, if you like.

Chocolate pancakes with maple banana

20 mins

food swaps

Use your favourite berries instead of cherries.

keep it

Pancakes can be frozen for up to 1 month.

---

2 tablespoons vegetable oil
2 small bananas (260g)
2 tablespoons pure maple syrup, plus extra to serve
½ cup (140g) coconut yoghurt
100g (3oz) fresh cherries

pancake batter

1¼ cups (185g) self-raising flour
2 tablespoons dutch-processed cocoa
½ teaspoon bicarbonate of soda (baking soda)
½ teaspoon ground cinnamon
¾ cup (180ml) almond milk
2 teaspoons apple cider vinegar
⅓ cup (80ml) pure maple syrup

---

1 Make pancake batter.

2 Heat a large, non-stick frying pan over medium heat; brush with a little oil. Pour ¼ cups of the pancake batter into pan; cook pancakes, in batches, for 2 minutes or until bubbles appear on the surface. Turn pancakes; cook for a further 1 minute or until lightly browned. Remove from pan; cover to keep warm. Repeat with remaining oil and batter to make 8 pancakes in total. Reserve pan.

3 Slice bananas on a sharp angle. Place reserved pan over medium-high heat. Add maple syrup and bananas to hot pan; cook for 2 minutes or until caramelised, turn and cook for a further 30 seconds.

4 Serve pancakes topped with coconut yoghurt, caramelised bananas, cherries and extra maple syrup.

pancake batter

Sift flour, cocoa, bicarbonate of soda and cinnamon into a medium bowl. Whisk milk, vinegar and maple syrup together in a small jug. Make a well in the centre of flour. Gradually pour in almond milk mixture, while whisking until a smooth batter forms; stand for 5 minutes.

No-egg spinach & tomato omelette

serves 2

 20 mins

 vegan hacks

There are various nut-based vegan fettas available in the market place to choose from. Our favourite is made from macadamias. You could also use other vegan cheeses or crumbled tempeh or tofu.

300g (9½oz) silken tofu
2 tablespoons extra virgin olive oil
⅓ cup (80ml) soy milk
⅓ cup (50g) chickpea flour (besan)
2 tablespoons nutritional yeast flakes
½ teaspoon sea salt flakes
¼ teaspoon ground turmeric

spinach filling

120g (4oz) spinach leaf salad mix
1 shallot, sliced thinly
200g (6½oz) heirloom cherry tomatoes, sliced or halved
1 tablespoon red wine vinegar
2 tablespoons extra virgin olive oil
60g (2oz) drained marinated vegan fetta (see vegan hacks)

1 Pat tofu dry with paper towel. Blend tofu with 1 tablespoon of the oil and remaining ingredients in a blender until smooth.

2 Heat a 22cm (9in) non-stick frying pan over high heat. Add 2 teaspoons of the oil; reduce heat to medium-high. Add half the tofu mixture; swirl or spread mixture until base is covered. Cook for 3 minutes or until small bubbles appear on surface. Slide omelette onto a warm plate; cover to keep warm. Repeat with remaining oil and tofu mixture to make a second omelette; slide onto a second warm plate.

3 Make spinach filling.

4 Divide filling between omelettes, placing it over half of each omelette; fold over. Serve immediately.

spinach filling

Place spinach mix, shallot, tomatoes, vinegar and oil in a medium bowl; toss gently to combine. Top with fetta.

Brekkie break

Start your day with these bircher bowls full of flavour

These bircher recipes make the perfect brekkie for those with a busy lifestyle. Simply prepare in a air-tight container the night before and grab it as you run out the door.

Super seed bircher

prep time 15 minutes (+ refrigeration) **serves** 4

Crumble ½ cup coconut flakes into a medium bowl. Stir in ⅓ cup sunflower seeds, ⅓ cup pepitas (pumpkin seed kernels), ¼ cup white chia seeds, ¼ cup linseed meal (flaxmeal) and 1¼ cups almond milk; cover, refrigerate for at least 1 hour or overnight. Cut 2 medium (300g) green apples into matchsticks and thickly slice 200g (6oz) strawberries. Divide seed mixture among serving bowls; top with apple and strawberry. Drizzle with coconut nectar syrup or pure maple syrup.

Make-and-go bircher

prep time 10 minutes **serves** 2

Cut 1 large (230g) ripe banana in half. Place each half in a 2-cup (500ml) glass jar; coarsely mash with a fork. Cut 1 large (200g) red apple, with the skin on, into matchsticks; divide between jars. Add ½ cup rolled oats and a pinch of ground cinnamon. Top each jar with 1 tablespoon pepitas (pumpkin seed kernels) and 2 tablespoons blueberries. Stir ¾ cup almond and coconut milk into each jar. Seal and go.

Pomegranate & pear bircher

prep time 15 minutes (+ refrigeration) **serves** 6

Combine 2 cups almond milk and 1 cup pomegranate juice in a medium bowl. Add 1 cup rolled oats, ½ cup quinoa flakes and 2 tablespoons white chia seeds; stir to combine. Grate 1 large (330g) pear, add to oat mixture; stir to combine. Cover; refrigerate for 3 hours or overnight. Divide bircher among bowls, drizzle with pure maple syrup. Top each serving with 1 tablespoon pomegranate seeds, sliced pear and a little grated orange rind.

tip Pomegranate seeds (arils) are sold in small punnets in the fresh food section at supermarkets.

Tropical coconut bircher

prep time 15 minutes **serves** 4

Combine 3 cups quinoa flakes, 1 cup coconut milk, 1 cup coconut water and 1 cup cloudy apple juice in a medium bowl. Divide bircher among four bowls. Cut 1 small (250g) dragon fruit and 1 small (300g) mango into slices; divide fruit among bowls. Serve bircher topped with the pulp of 1 passionfruit and ¼ cup coconut flakes.

Caramelised mangoes with coconut

serves 4

1 cup (50g) flaked coconut
4 small mangoes (1.2kg)
½ cup (135g) grated dark palm
sugar, plus extra to serve
2 cups (560g) coconut yoghurt
1 cup (150g) roasted salted
macadamias, chopped

1 Stir coconut in a small frying pan over low-medium heat for 3 minutes or until lightly toasted. Remove from pan.

2 Remove cheeks from mangoes, then cut parallel lines into the flesh side of each half.

3 Heat a heavy-based frying pan (or chargrill pan) over high heat. Sprinkle cut sides of mango with palm sugar; place, cut-side down, in pan for 2 minutes or until sugar caramelises.

4 Divide mango halves among plates; top with yoghurt, toasted coconut and macadamias. Serve sprinkled with extra palm sugar.

 15 mins

 food swaps

Brown sugar instead of the palm sugar.

 serving ideas

Serve topped with freshly grated lime rind or mint leaves.

TIP The flesh that is left around the stone of the mango can be cut off and frozen in zip-top bags for smoothies.

Apple pie spiced oats

serves 4

 25 mins

 serving ideas

Add coarsely chopped pecans to the caramelised apple mixture for the last 2 minutes of cooking, if you like.

3 medium pink lady or other red apples (450g)
70g (2½oz) vegan margarine
⅓ cup (75g) firmly packed brown sugar
½ teaspoon ground cinnamon
1¼ cups (120g) rolled oats
1 litre (4 cups) vanilla-flavoured almond milk

1 Cut 2 unpeeled apples crossways into 4 thick slices. Heat 30g (1oz) vegan margarine in a medium, deep frying pan over medium heat; cook apple slices and ¼ cup of brown sugar, turning, for 7 minutes or until caramelised and tender. Remove apples from pan; reserve syrup.

2 Grate remaining unpeeled apple. Return frying pan to medium heat. Add remaining vegan margarine, grated apple and cinnamon; cook, stirring for 2 minutes. Add oats, remaining sugar and 3½ cups of the almond milk; bring to the boil. Reduce heat to low; cook, stirring, for 5 minutes or until oats are cooked and mixture thickened.

3 Spoon porridge into bowls; top with apple slices and reserved syrup. Serve with remaining almond milk.

TIPS

Add ¼ teaspoon vanilla extract with plain almond milk in step 2, if you like. You could use any vegan milk you prefer.

Blueberry pie brekkie pops

250g (8oz) fresh or frozen
   blueberries
1 teaspoon ground cinnamon
⅓ cup (80ml) pure maple syrup
½ teaspoon finely grated lemon rind
1½ cups (180g) muesli
1 cup (280g) coconut yoghurt

 **25
mins**

**(+ refrigeration
& freezing)**

1 Stir blueberries, cinnamon and 2 tablespoons of the syrup in a small saucepan over high heat; bring to the boil. Reduce heat to medium; simmer, mashing blueberries occasionally with a wooden spoon, for 5 minutes or until liquid is thickened slightly. Stir in rind. Transfer to a small bowl; refrigerate for 20 minutes or until cooled slightly.

2 Meanwhile, blend or process muesli until it resembles fine crumbs. Transfer to a small bowl, stir in remaining syrup.

3 Fold muesli mixture and yoghurt through blueberry mixture. Spoon yoghurt mixture into eight ⅓-cup (80ml) popsicle moulds, pressing down firmly.

4 Freeze pops for 2 hours or until firm enough to hold sticks upright. Insert sticks, making sure the sticks are centred.

5 Freeze popsicles for a further 4 hours or overnight until firm.

TIPS
You can use your favourite muesli for this recipe. Dip the moulds in warm water for 5 seconds to loosen. If your popsicle mould includes sticks that stay in place, insert them in step 4 then freeze for 6 hours or overnight until firm; disregard step 5.

Grilled fruit salad & coconut yoghurt

 15 mins

1 medium pear (230g), cored, cut into 8 wedges

4 medium figs (240g), halved lengthways

1 medium blood orange (240g), peeled, cut into 1cm (½in) thick slices

⅓ cup (95g) coconut yoghurt

3 teaspoons sunflower seeds, toasted

1 Cook pear on a heated lightly oiled grill plate (or grill or barbecue), over medium-high heat, for 4 minutes each side or until slightly tender and charred. Add figs halfway through cooking time (see tip); cook for 2 minutes each side until figs are tender and charred.

2 Serve grilled fruit and orange slices in serving bowls, topped with coconut yoghurt and sunflower seeds.

TIPS

To cook figs, place a small sheet of baking paper on the grill plate to prevent the figs from sticking. For an on-the-go breakfast, you could eat this fruit salad fresh without grilling the fruit.

Orange & vanilla rawnola

makes 2½ cups

1 cup (90g) rolled oats
12 fresh dates (240g), pitted
½ cup (40g) shredded coconut
2 teaspoons finely grated
  orange rind
1 teaspoon vanilla bean paste

1 Place ingredients in a food processor; pulse until they start to clump together. (Do not over-process or the mixture will form a ball.)

2 Transfer rawnola to an airtight container. Store in the fridge for up to 2 weeks.

flavour variations

fig + almond rawnola Swap dates with dried figs and coconut with almonds.

apricot + walnut rawnola Swap dates with dried apricots and coconut with walnuts.

apple + brazil nut rawnola Swap dates with dried apple and coconut with brazil nuts.

 10 mins

 vegan hacks

For bliss balls, process the mixture until it comes together then roll tablespoons of mixture into balls.

 serving ideas

Serve rawnola with sliced banana, vegan yoghurt, strips of orange rind and ground cinnamon as a substantial meal or on its own as a snack.

Coconut quinoa pudding

 25 mins

(+ standing)

 food swaps

Use lemongrass or the finely grated rind of 1 lemon or lime instead of kaffir lime leaves.

🍽 **serving ideas**

Serve topped with passionfruit.

1 cup (200g) white quinoa
2 medium ripe bananas (400g)
50g (1½oz) palm sugar, plus extra, grated to serve
1 litre (4 cups) rice and coconut milk blend (see tip)
6 fresh kaffir lime leaves
¼ teaspoon fine sea salt

1 Place quinoa in a heatproof bowl with enough warm tap water to just cover; stand for 15 minutes. Drain.

2 Meanwhile, mash 1 banana with a fork in a small bowl; finely grate palm sugar into the bowl.

3 Reserve ½ cup milk blend for serving. Place remaining milk blend in a saucepan with drained quinoa, mashed banana mixture, 4 whole lime leaves and salt; bring to the boil. Reduce heat to low; simmer, covered, stirring occasionally, for 20 minutes or until quinoa is tender. Discard lime leaves.

4 Meanwhile, cut out and discard centre stems from remaining lime leaves. Roll up leaves; shred finely. Slice remaining banana.

5 Spoon warm pudding into small bowls, top with sliced banana and shredded lime leaves. Drizzle with reserved milk blend; sprinkle with a little extra grated palm sugar.

TIP

We used Coco Quench, a rice and coconut milk blend sold in most supermarkets. You could also create your own blend with rice and coconut milk, or almond and coconut milk.

Pea spread & fermented veg on toast

serves 4

15 mins

vegan hacks

Sprouted bread is available from some health food stores, gourmet food stores and markets; keep refrigerated. Alternatively, you can use any bread you like for this recipe.

keep it

Pea spread can be kept in an airtight container in the fridge for up to 1 day.

3 cups (360g) frozen peas
⅓ cup (90g) hulled tahini
2 tablespoons fresh dill leaves
1 clove garlic, crushed
2 tablespoons lemon juice
1 tablespoon dijon mustard
2 tablespoons sunflower seeds
2 teaspoons sesame seeds
2 teaspoons linseeds (flaxseed)
9 x 80g (1½lb total) slices sprouted bread, toasted (see vegan hacks)
1⅓ cups (240g) drained store-bought fermented vegetables of choice
1 cup (15g) loosely packed snow pea tendrils
lemon wedges, to serve

1 Place peas in a heatproof bowl; cover with boiling water. Stand for 2 minutes; drain. Blend or process peas, tahini, dill, garlic, juice and mustard until it forms a chunky spread. Season to taste.

2 Place seeds in a small heavy-based frying pan; stir seeds constantly over medium-high heat until browned.

3 Top toasted bread with spread, vegetables, seeds and snow pea tendrils. Serve with lemon wedges.

Light lunches

Scrambled tofu & avocado wraps

 20 mins

 do ahead

The recipe is best made close to serving.

 serving ideas

Add corn kernels to the wrap, if you like. Process the chopped avocado until smooth for a guacamole-style spread instead.

600g (1¼lb) firm tofu
1 tablespoon olive oil
1 tablespoon tamari
30g (1oz) baby spinach, sliced thinly
1 large tomato (220g), chopped
2 green onions (scallions), chopped finely
1 cup (240g) canned refried beans with chilli
4 x 21cm (8½in) red quinoa wraps or tortillas (100g)
1 medium avocado (250g), chopped
⅓ cup coriander (cilantro) leaves
hot chilli sauce, to taste
lime wedges, to serve

1 Pat tofu dry with paper towel. Crumble tofu into pieces with your fingers.

2 Heat the oil in a large frying pan over medium heat; cook tofu and tamari, stirring, for 2 minutes or until warmed through. Add spinach, tomato and green onion and cook for 1 minute. Season to taste. Remove from pan; cover to keep warm.

3 Stir beans in a small saucepan over low heat until hot. Spread beans on wraps; top with tofu mixture, avocado, coriander and sauce. Roll up to enclose fillings. Serve with lime wedges.

TIP

If you prefer a milder flavour, you can use a brand of plain refried beans and omit the hot chilli sauce. The beans can be heated in the microwave.

serves
2

Tofu poke bowl

 20 mins

 vegan hacks

Check ingredients listed on the miso as some brands contain bonito (tuna) extract which is unsuitable for vegans.

2 tablespoons rice wine vinegar
1 teaspoon white (shiro) miso (see vegan hacks)
¼ teaspoon shichimi togarashi
250g (8oz) block firm tofu, sliced
1 tablespoon olive oil
3 radishes (105g)
½ sheet nori (seaweed), toasted, shredded
½ small lebanese cucumber (65g), thinly sliced
¼ cup (40g) frozen edamame (soybeans), thawed, shelled
½ medium ripe avocado (125g), sliced
toasted sesame seeds, to serve (optional)

poke rice base

2 x 450g (14½oz) packets microwave brown rice
⅓ cup (80ml) tamari
⅓ cup (80ml) lime juice
1 tablespoon extra virgin olive oil
1½ teaspoons sesame oil
3 teaspoons finely grated fresh ginger
2 cloves garlic, crushed
pinch chilli flakes

1 Combine vinegar, miso and shichimi togarashi in a small bowl. Add sliced tofu, toss to combine. Set aside for 10 minutes.

2 Meanwhile, make poke rice base.

3 Heat oil in a large non-stick frying pan over medium heat, cook tofu for 30 seconds on each side or until browned. Divide tofu evenly between rice plates.

4 Julienne 2 of the radishes; quarter the remaining radish. Top rice plates with radish, seaweed, cucumber, edamame and avocado; sprinkle with sesame seeds. Serve immediately.

poke rice base

Heat microwave rice following packet directions. Combine tamari, juice, oils, ginger, garlic and chilli flakes in a small bowl. Add rice, toss to combine. Divide between two plates.

Sprout & coriander salad

⏳ **20 mins**

🕐 **do ahead**

The dressing discolours quickly, so make it close to serving. Prepare the remaining ingredients several hours ahead and refrigerate separately.

2 tablespoons sunflower seeds
2 tablespoons pepitas (pumpkin seed kernels)
½ bunch coriander (cilantro)
3 green onions (scallions), sliced thinly
¼ cup (60ml) extra virgin olive oil
¼ cup (60ml) lime juice
¼ teaspoon ground coriander
¼ teaspoon ground cumin
2 lebanese cucumbers (260g)
2 medium roma (plum) tomatoes (150g), cut into wedges
400g (12½oz) crunchy combo sprouted legumes

1 Stir seeds in a small dry frying pan over medium heat until toasted lightly. Cool to room temperature.

2 To make the coriander dressing, wash coriander well; drain and pat dry. Reserve 1 cup leaves. Scrape and clean coriander roots. Blend or process coriander roots, stems and remaining coriander leaves with one-third each of the green onion, oil, juice and spices until chopped finely. Season to taste.

3 Halve cucumbers, remove seeds; slice thinly on the diagonal.

4 Place cucumber, tomato, sprouts, seeds, remaining green onion and coriander dressing in a large bowl. Add remaining oil, juice and spices; toss to combine. Top with reserved coriander leaves. Season to taste; serve immediately.

serves 4

Beetroot & pistachio crumble subs

15 mins

food swaps

Use almonds, walnuts, hazelnuts or pepitas instead of pistachios.

vegan hacks

Vacuum-packed cooked beetroot is available in the fresh food section in most large supermarkets.

1 small baguette (300g)
½ cup (150g) vegan mayonnaise
1½ teaspoons bottled grated horseradish
⅓ cup (45g) pistachios, chopped
2 tablespoons thyme leaves
1 tablespoon chopped chives
1 teaspoon finely grated lemon rind
250g (8oz) vacuum-packed cooked beetroot (beets), cut into rounds
2 teaspoons balsamic glaze
lemon cheeks, to serve
micro herbs, to serve (optional)

1 Preheat a chargrill pan (or grill/broiler) to high. Split baguette in half horizontally, then cut each half into 10cm (4in) lengths. Chargrill bread pieces for 2 minutes on each side or until grill marks appear.

2 Combine mayonnaise and horseradish in a small bowl; season.

3 Combine pistachios, thyme, chives and lemon rind in a small bowl. Season well.

4 Spread mayonnaise mixture over baguette halves. Top with beetroot slices and pistachio mixture. Drizzle with balsamic glaze and serve with lemon cheeks and micro herbs.

makes 10

Pea, miso & mint rice paper rolls

30 mins

vegan hacks

Check ingredients listed on the miso as some brands contain bonito (tuna) extract which is unsuitable for vegans.

keep it

Best made on day of serving. Make a few hours ahead, then store, covered with damp paper towel in an airtight container in the fridge.

2 cups (240g) frozen peas, thawed
1 medium avocado (250g), chopped coarsely
1 tablespoon white (shiro) miso (see vegan hacks)
1 teaspoon finely grated lime rind
1 tablespoon lime juice
¼ cup coarsely chopped fresh mint leaves
10 x 22cm (9in) rice papers rounds
2 cups (160g) finely shredded purple cabbage
2 cups julienned daikon
1 teaspoon black sesame seeds
pickled ginger, to serve

1 Process peas, avocado, miso, lime rind, juice and mint until well combined but not quite smooth. Season to taste.

2 Place one rice paper round in a medium bowl of lukewarm water for 15 seconds or until just soft. Place on a clean tea towel or paper towel. Repeat with remaining rice paper rounds.

3 Place 1 tablespoon of the cabbage on the centre of each rice paper round, top with 2 tablespoons pea mixture; divide remaining cabbage and daikon among rice paper wrappers. Fold edges in and roll up firmly to enclose fillings. Sprinkle rolls with sesame seeds. Serve with pickled ginger.

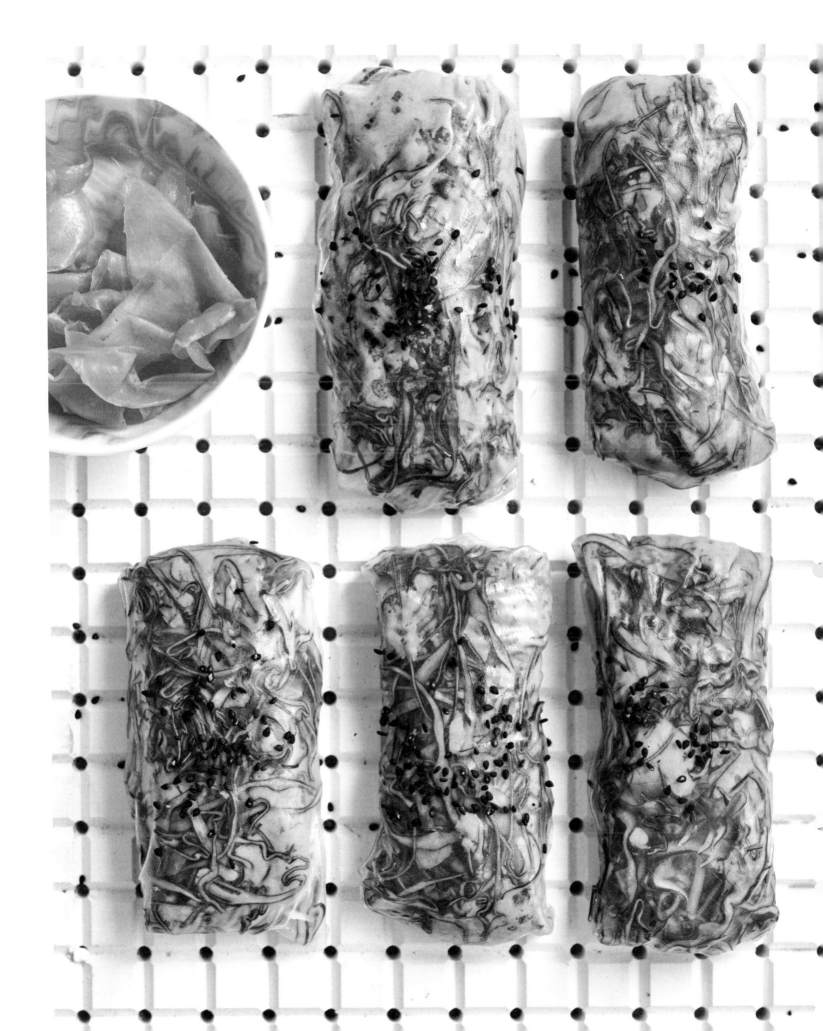

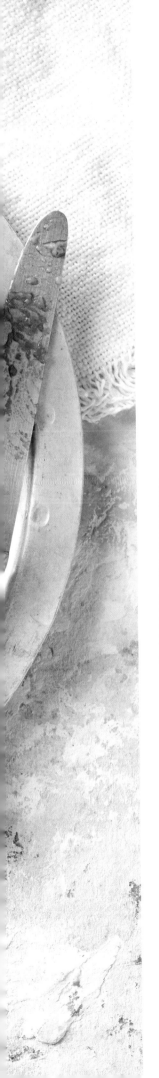

makes 4

Char-grilled vegie & pumpkin wrap

10 mins

food swaps

Use your favourite style of wrap. Use bread rolls instead, if you prefer.

vegan hacks

Check the wrap packet label to ensure the brand is vegan.

2 x 280g (9oz) jars char-grilled vegetables
200g (8oz) tub dairy-free moroccan pumpkin dip
4 large wraps (200g)
40g (1½oz) baby rocket (arugula) leaves

1 Drain char-grilled vegetables; pat dry with paper towel, season to taste.

2 Spread pumpkin dip onto wraps; top evenly with char-grilled vegetables and rocket. Roll to enclose fillings.

Fresh samosa wraps

30 mins

food swaps

Use orange sweet potato and different varieties of wraps and chutney.

keep it

The potato mixture will keep refrigerated for up to 3 days.

1 large potato (300g), peeled, cut into 1cm (½in) pieces
2 tablespoons extra virgin olive oil
½ cup (60g) frozen peas
2 teaspoons curry powder
2 red quinoa wraps (90g)
2 tablespoons vegan mayonnaise
30g (1oz) baby spinach leaves
1 lebanese cucumber (130g), thinly sliced lengthways
½ small red onion (50g), sliced thinly
⅓ cup coriander (cilantro)
2 tablespoons mango chutney
lime wedges, to serve

1 Boil, steam or microwave potato until just tender; drain.

2 Heat oil in a medium frying pan over high heat; cook potato, peas and curry powder, stirring, for 3 minutes or until potatoes are slightly mashed and peas are hot.

3 Spread wraps with mayonnaise, top with spinach leaves, cucumber, onion, coriander, potato mixture and chutney. Roll up to enclose filling. Serve with lime wedges.

TIPS

You can enjoy these wraps either hot or cold. For cold wraps, allow the potato filling to cool completely before assembling. Cover the assembled wraps in plastic wrap and refrigerate until ready to eat.

serves 4

Spicy chickpea & yoghurt dipping jars

25 mins

food swaps

Try other legumes in this recipe, such as white beans or four bean mix.

serving ideas

Serve these salad jars with crispbreads or chargrilled slices of wholegrain bread as dippers.

2 cups (560g) vegan yoghurt
½ cup finely chopped dill leaves
2 cloves garlic, crushed
½ cup (125ml) lemon juice
2 x 400g (12½oz) can chickpeas (garbanzo beans), drained, rinsed (see food swaps)
⅓ cup (55g) currants
150g (4½oz) drained char-grilled capsicum (bell pepper), sliced thinly
1 small red onion (100g), quartered, sliced thinly
2 lebanese cucumbers (260g), chopped finely
½ cup (70g) slivered almonds, toasted
2 teaspoons harissa paste
2 tablespoons olive oil

1 Combine yoghurt, dill, half the garlic and 2 tablespoons of the juice in a small bowl. Season to taste.

2 Combine chickpeas, currants, capsicum, onion, cucumber and ⅓ cup of the almonds in a medium bowl.

3 Combine harissa, oil and remaining garlic and juice in a small bowl.

4 Spoon yoghurt mixture into four 1½ cup (375ml) jars. Top with salad, a spoonful of harissa dressing and remaining almonds.

Winter veg with miso peanut dressing

20 mins

serving ideas

For a more substantial meal, you can add sliced teriyaki-flavoured or plain tofu.

vegan hacks

Check ingredients listed on the miso as some brands contain bonito (tuna) extract which is unsuitable for vegans.

1 baby fennel bulb (130g)
1 medium beetroot (beet) (150g)
400g (12½oz) baby carrots
1 cup (80g) finely shredded red cabbage
1 cup (80g) finely shredded green cabbage
⅓ cup (45g) finely chopped roasted unsalted peanuts
½ cup mint leaves
lime wedges, to serve

miso peanut dressing

½ cup (140g) crunchy natural peanut butter
¼ cup (70g) white (shiro) miso (see vegan hacks)
2 tablespoons coconut sugar
½ teaspoon finely grated lime rind
1 fresh small red chilli, chopped finely
⅓ cup (80ml) lime juice

1 Make miso peanut dressing.

2 Thinly slice fennel bulb and stems. Peel beetroot, cut into matchsticks. Trim carrots, peel into ribbons.

3 Divide fennel, beetroot, carrots and cabbage between bowls, top with peanuts and mint. Serve with dressing and lime wedges.

miso peanut dressing

Blend or process ingredients with ½ cup (125ml) water until combined.

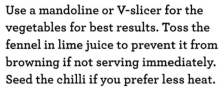

TIP Use a mandoline or V-slicer for the vegetables for best results. Toss the fennel in lime juice to prevent it from browning if not serving immediately. Seed the chilli if you prefer less heat.

serves
4

Tempeh chips with lentil salad

25 mins

food swaps

You can use other leafy greens like kale, silverbeet (swiss chard) or spinach instead of cavolo nero.

vegan hacks

Tempeh can be found in the refrigerator section of some large supermarkets and health food stores.

1¾ cups (350g) French-style dried green lentils
10 cavolo nero (tuscan cabbage) leaves (100g), trimmed, shredded
400g (12½oz) mixed cherry tomato medley, halved
1 small red onion (80g), quartered, sliced thinly
¼ cup small basil leaves
¼ cup mint leaves
¼ cup flat-leaf parsley leaves
½ cup (125ml) olive oil
¼ cup (60ml) red wine vinegar
2 teaspoons dijon mustard

tempeh chips

¼ cup (60ml) olive oil
100g (3oz) tempeh, cut into 3mm (⅛in) slices

1 Cook lentils in a large saucepan of boiling water for 12 minutes or until just tender; drain. Rinse under cold water; drain well.

2 Meanwhile, make tempeh chips.

3 Arrange lentils, cavolo nero, tomato, onion and herbs on plates or trays.

4 Place oil, vinegar and mustard in a screw-top jar; shake well. Season.

5 Serve salad with tempeh chips and dressing in small bowls to the side.

tempeh chips

Heat oil in a large frying pan over medium-high heat; cook tempeh for 1 minute each side or until golden. Drain on paper towel.

TIP French-style green lentils are related to the famous French lentils du puy; these green-blue, tiny lentils have a nutty, earthy flavour and a hardy nature that allows them to be rapidly cooked without disintegrating.

Mushroom & spinach gozleme

makes 4

 15 mins

 vegan hacks

If you have one, you can cook the gozleme in a sandwich press.

⅓ cup (80ml) extra virgin olive oil
1 small onion (80g), chopped finely
2 cloves garlic, crushed
2 teaspoons ground cumin
2 teaspoons ground sumac
½ teaspoon chilli flakes
350g (11oz) flat mushrooms, sliced thickly
100g (3oz) vegan cheddar, grated
60g (2oz) spinach leaves
2 tablespoons pine nuts, toasted
4 mountain bread wraps (100g)
olive oil cooking spray
mint leaves and lemon wedges, to serve

1 Heat 1 tablespoon of the oil in a large frying pan over high; cook onion and garlic, stirring, for 5 minutes or until softened. Stir in cumin, sumac and chilli flakes; cook for 1 minute. Transfer mixture to a bowl.

2 Heat 1½ tablespoons of the oil in same frying pan. Add half the mushrooms; cook, turning occasionally, for 5 minutes or until golden. Add cooked mushrooms to onion mixture. Repeat with remaining oil and mushrooms. Cool combined mixture for 10 minutes. Stir in vegan cheddar, spinach and pine nuts; season to taste.

3 Heat a large frying pan over high heat. Place two mountain bread wraps on a work bench. Spread a quarter of the filling mixture down the centre third of each wrap. Fold both sides over to enclose. Spray with olive oil cooking spray. Cook in the pan for 2 minutes each side or until cheddar melts and bread is crisp. Remove from pan, using a large spatula. Cover to keep warm. Repeat with remaining mountain bread wraps and filling, spraying with olive oil.

4 Cut each gozleme diagonally and serve with mint and lemon wedges.

serves 2

Tamari noodle salad jars

20 mins

food swaps

If you don't have kimchi, toss the shredded cabbage in 1 teaspoon rice wine vinegar before layering.

vegan hacks

If you're not preparing the recipe ahead of time, add the ingredients directly into a bowl in step 3 and mix to combine.

100g (3oz) dried rice stick noodles
250g (8oz) firm tofu, cubed
1 cup (80g) finely shredded red cabbage
2 small carrots (140g), julienned or grated
2 tablespoons vegan kimchi
1 cup (80g) bean sprouts
½ cup coriander (cilantro) leaves
½ cup mint leaves

sesame dressing

6cm (2½in) fresh ginger
2 tablespoons tamari
1 tablespoon sesame oil
1 tablespoon extra virgin olive oil
1 tablespoon rice wine vinegar

1 Cook noodles in a medium saucepan of boiling water for 6 minutes or until tender. Drain; rinse under running cold water.

2 Make sesame dressing.

3 Place tofu cubes into two 3½ cup (875ml) jars with a lid; pour dressing over tofu. Layer with the cabbage, carrot, noodles, kimchi and bean sprouts, then top with herbs. Cover jars with the lid. Refrigerate until ready to eat.

4 To serve, pour contents into a bowl and toss to combine.

sesame dressing

Peel and finely grate ginger. Squeeze the grated ginger in your hand over a small bowl to extract juice; you should have approximately 1 teaspoon ginger juice. Discard ginger pulp. Add remaining ingredients to bowl; mix to combine.

serves 4

Greek salad with nut fetta

 30 mins

 food swaps

We used green zebra tomatoes, but you can use any type.

1 tablespoon extra virgin olive oil
1 clove garlic, crushed
400g (12½oz) can butter beans, drained, rinsed
1 teaspoon dried chilli flakes
2 baby cos (romaine) lettuce (400g), trimmed, quartered
500g (1lb) mixed green heirloom tomatoes, sliced
200g (6½oz) baby cucumbers, sliced lengthways, chopped
1 medium yellow capsicum (bell pepper) (200g), seeded, sliced
½ cup (80g) pitted kalamata olives, torn
120g (4oz) marinated almond or macadamia fetta
¼ cup fresh oregano leaves

oregano dressing
¼ cup (60ml) extra virgin olive oil
1 tablespoon white wine vinegar
2 tablespoons lemon juice
1 small clove garlic, crushed
1 teaspoon dried oregano
½ teaspoon caster (superfine) sugar

1 Make oregano dressing.

2 Heat oil in a medium frying pan over medium-high heat; cook garlic and beans for 5 minutes, stirring occasionally, or until beans are starting to brown and crisp. Remove from heat; sprinkle with chilli flakes, cool in pan.

3 Arrange lettuce, bean mixture, tomatoes, cucumber and capsicum on a large platter or individual plates; top with olives and fetta.

4 Drizzle salad with dressing and scatter with oregano leaves.

oregano dressing
Place ingredients in a screw-top jar; shake very well. Season to taste.

serves 4

Green mango slaw with chilli-lime dressing

 25 mins

 vegan hacks

Leftover slaw can be used in the Marinated tofu bánh mì rolls on page 78.

¼ medium red cabbage (330g), sliced thinly
1 large carrot (180g), peeled, cut into matchsticks
1 large green mango (800g), peeled, cut into matchsticks
5 shallots, sliced thinly
1 cup (150g) frozen shelled edamame (soybeans), thawed
⅓ cup mint leaves
⅓ cup thai basil leaves
¼ cup (40g) white sesame seeds, toasted

chilli-lime dressing

⅓ cup (80ml) lime juice
2 tablespoons grapeseed oil
1 tablespoon tamari
30g (1oz) palm sugar, grated finely
2 fresh long red chillies, seeded, chopped finely

1 Place cabbage, carrot, green mango, shallots, edamame, herbs and sesame seeds in a large bowl.

2 Make chilli-lime dressing.

3 Just before serving, drizzle dressing over salad; toss gently to combine.

chilli-lime dressing

Place ingredients in a screw-top jar; shake well until sugar dissolves. Season to taste.

Marinated tofu bánh mì rolls

makes 2

150g (4½oz) coleslaw salad mix
¼ cup fresh coriander (cilantro) leaves
¼ cup (75g) vegan mayonnaise
2 teaspoons rice wine vinegar
½ teaspoon sesame oil
½ teaspoon sea salt flakes
1 teaspoon olive oil
200g (6½oz) satay marinated tofu (see vegan hacks)
2 long white crusty bread rolls (140g)

1 Place coleslaw salad mix and coriander in a medium bowl. Combine 1 tablespoon of the vegan mayonnaise, the rice wine vinegar, sesame oil and salt in a small bowl. Add dressing to coleslaw mixture; toss to coat well.

2 Heat oil in a medium frying pan over medium-high heat; cook marinated tofu for 2 minutes, on each side, or until golden and heated through.

3 Split bread rolls in half; spread both sides with remaining mayonnaise. Fill with tofu and coleslaw mixture.

 15 mins

 food swaps

Use your favourite Asian-style marinated tofu instead of the satay.

 vegan hacks

To make your own satay marinated tofu, combine 2 tablespoons crunchy peanut butter, 1 tablespoon kecap manis and 2 teaspoons peanut oil with 200g (6½oz) thickly sliced firm tofu; refrigerate for 20 minutes before cooking.

Raw vegie nori rolls

makes 12

 20 mins

1 cup (150g) sunflower seeds
3 green onions (scallions),
    sliced thinly
¼ cup coriander (cilantro) leaves
¼ cup (60ml) lemon juice
2 tablespoons tamari, plus extra
    to serve
1 clove garlic
6 sheets nori (seaweed) (15g),
    halved
¼ small red cabbage (200g),
    sliced finely
1 large carrot (180g),
    cut into matchsticks
4 baby cucumbers (120g),
    sliced lengthways
½ cup (20g) alfalfa sprouts

1 Place sunflower seeds in a medium bowl with enough cold water to cover. Stand for 10 minutes. Drain, rinse under cold water; drain well.

2 Process soaked sunflower seeds with green onions, coriander, lemon juice, tamari, garlic, and ¼ cup (60ml) water until it forms a chunky paste.

3 Place a half nori sheet on a clean work bench. Spread one corner with 1 tablespoon of sunflower mixture, top with one-twelfth of the red cabbage, carrot, cucumber and alfalfa sprouts. Fold nori sheet over vegetables, and roll sheet away from you on a diagonal to form a cone. Dampen the edge of the nori sheet with water to seal and close. Repeat with remaining ingredients to make 12 rolls. Serve rolls with extra tamari.

Beer battered potato scallops with minty dip

serves 4

 30 mins

500g (1lb) potatoes
250g (8oz) orange sweet potatoes
400g (12½oz) frozen shelled
  edamame (soybeans)
½ cup finely chopped mint
1 clove garlic, crushed
⅓ cup (80ml) tahini
¼ cup (60ml) lemon juice
vegetable oil, for deep-frying
1 cup (150g) plain (all-purpose)
  flour
1¼ cups (310ml) lager beer
malt vinegar and lemon wedges,
  to serve

1 Peel potatoes and sweet potatoes; cut into 1cm (½in) thick slices. Cook potatoes together in a saucepan of boiling water for 3 minutes. Drain well; pat dry with paper towel. Cool.

2 Meanwhile, cook edamame in a medium saucepan of boiling water for 5 minutes; drain well. Place edamame in a food processor with mint, garlic, tahini, lemon juice and ½ cup (125ml) water; process until well combined. Season to taste.

3 Fill a large saucepan one-third full with oil; heat to 180°C/350°F (or until a small cube of bread turns golden in 15 seconds).

4 Whisk flour and beer in a medium bowl until smooth; season.

5 Dip potato slices in batter, allowing excess to drain off. Deep-fry, in two batches, for 5 minutes or until potato are tender, golden and crisp. Drain on paper towel. Sprinkle with salt.

6 Serve hot potato scallops with minty edamame, vinegar and lemon wedges.

TIPS

Try to use potatoes and sweet potatoes that are the same diameter as each another. Keep the first batch of potato scallops warm on an oven tray in a 180°C/350°F oven while you cook the second batch.

serves 2

Grains & greens goodness bowl

 20 mins

 food swaps

Swap the packet microwave brown rice and quinoa for any other grain and pulse mix.

⅓ cup (80ml) extra virgin olive oil
1 clove garlic, crushed
250g (8oz) packet microwave brown rice and quinoa
300g (9½oz) brussels sprouts, trimmed, halved
150g (4½oz) cavolo nero (tuscan kale), trimmed
1 medium avocado (250g), sliced
¼ cup (50g) pepitas (pumpkin seed kernels), toasted
1 tablespoon fresh basil leaves

tahini dressing

2 tablespoons tahini
¼ cup fresh basil leaves
3 teaspoons white wine vinegar

1 Make tahini dressing.

2 Heat 2 tablespoons of the oil in a large frying pan over medium-high heat. Add garlic; cook for 30 seconds. Add rice and quinoa mix; cook, stirring, for 5 minutes or until starting to crisp. Transfer rice mixture to a bowl; cover to keep warm.

3 Heat 1 tablespoon of the oil in same pan; cook brussels sprouts, turning occasionally, for 5 minutes or until charred and tender. Transfer to a plate; cover to keep warm.

4 Heat remaining oil in same pan; cook the cavolo nero, turning, for 2 minutes or until just starting to wilt. Transfer to plate; cover to keep warm.

5 Divide rice mixture between bowls; top with brussels sprouts, cavolo nero, avocado and pepitas. Drizzle with dressing and top with basil leaves. Serve with lemon wedges, if you like.

tahini dressing

Process ingredients with ½ cup (125ml) water in a small food processor until smooth. Season to taste.

Vego hotdogs

serves 2-6

Get your junk food fix with our quick & tasty not-dogs

Good quality vegan hotdogs can be bought from health food stores and most major supermarkets. Use slices of marinated tofu instead, if you like.

Bánh mì not-dog

prep + cook time 20 minutes

Cut 1 small (70g) carrot and 100g (3oz) piece daikon into julienne (matchsticks); place in a medium bowl with ¼ cup rice wine vinegar, season. Stand for 10 minutes. Meanwhile, combine ½ cup (150g) vegan mayonnaise and 1 teaspoon sriracha in a small bowl. Heat a large, lightly oiled frying pan over high heat; cook 4 vegan hotdogs (320g) for 5 minutes, turning, until browned. Warm 4 split long bread rolls (240g); spread with sriracha mayonnaise. Fill rolls with hotdogs. Drain carrot and daikon; place on hotdogs. Sprinkle with 1 thinly sliced green onion (scallion), ½ cup each fresh mint and coriander (cilantro) leaves and 2 tablespoons chopped roasted salted peanuts. Drizzle with extra sriracha to serve.

Reuben not-dog

prep + cook time 15 minutes

For the 'russian' dressing, combine ¼ cup vegan mayonnaise, ½ teaspoon tamarind puree (or A1 steak sauce) and 1 tablespoon each tomato sauce (ketchup), sweet mustard pickle and lemon juice in a small bowl. Heat a large, lightly oiled frying pan over high heat; cook 4 vegan hotdogs (320g) for 5 minutes, turning, until browned. Place 4 split long bread rolls (240g) on an oven tray; top with 150g (4½oz) sliced vegan cheddar. Place under a preheated grill (broiler) for 2 minutes or until cheese melts. Fill with hotdogs, ½ cup store-bought caramelised onions, ½ cup (40g) sauerkraut and ½ cup sliced dill pickles. Drizzle with dressing. Top with finely chopped dill sprigs, if you like.

Nacho not-dog

prep + cook time 15 minutes

Preheated grill (broiler) to high. Place 4 vegan hotdogs (320g) and 1 cup (190g) mexi beans in a large, non-stick frying pan over low heat; cook, turning hotdogs, for 3 minutes or until warm. Place 4 split long bread rolls (240g) rolls on an oven tray; fill rolls with 25g (¾oz) corn chips, then hotdogs and beans. Sprinkle with 1 cup grated vegan cheddar. Place under hot grill for 2 minutes or until cheese melts. Top with ⅓ cup pickled sliced jalapeño chillies and ¼ cup chopped coriander (cilantro).

Kimchi not-dog

prep + cook time 20 minutes

In a large bowl, combine 125g (4oz) shredded white cabbage, 1 thinly sliced green onion (scallion), ⅓ cup coarsely chopped fresh coriander (cilantro), 2 tablespoons lemon juice and ¼ teaspoon sesame oil. For sesame mayo, stir ¼ teaspoon sesame oil and ½ cup vegan mayonnaise in a small bowl; season. Heat a large, lightly oiled frying pan over high heat; cook 4 vegan hotdogs (320g) for 2 minutes. Add 1 cup (100g) chopped vegan kimchi; cook, turning, for a further 3 minutes or until warmed through. Warm 4 split long bread rolls (240g); spread with sesame mayo. Fill rolls with hotdogs and kimchi, then top with cabbage salad and 2 teaspoons toasted sesame seeds.

Tomato & rocket tarts

makes 8

2 sheets shortcrust pastry
   (see vegan hacks)
250g (8oz) baby tomatoes, sliced
50g (1½oz) baby rocket (arugula)
   leaves
1½ tablespoons balsamic vinegar

1 Preheat oven to 180°C/350°F. Line two oven trays with baking paper.

2 Cut pastry sheets into four squares each; place on trays. Fold edges of pastry over to form a 5mm (¼in) border; prick pastry bases with fork

3 Bake pastry bases for 15 minutes or until crisp.

4 Combine tomatoes, rocket and vinegar in large bowl. Spoon tomato mixture onto warm pastry bases.

20 mins

vegan hacks

Check the ingredients listed on the pastry packet label to ensure the brand is vegan.

Black beans & corn quesadillas

serves 4

⏳ **30 mins**

400g (12½oz) can black beans, drained, rinsed
1½ teaspoons smoked paprika
1 cup (120g) coarsely grated vegan cheddar
2 green onions (scallions), sliced thinly
8 x 15cm (6in) fresh white corn tortillas
lime wedges and micro coriander, to serve (optional)

1 Combine beans and paprika in a medium bowl; using the back of a fork, coarsely mash. Add cheddar and green onion; mix well, season.

2 Place four of the tortillas on a clean chopping board. Spoon bean mixture evenly over tortillas. Top with remaining tortillas.

3 Heat a medium frying pan over medium heat; cook one quesadilla at a time, pressing down firmly with a spatula, for 5 minutes or until the tortilla is crisp and golden brown. Turn over; cook for a further 3 minutes or until cheddar has melted and tortilla is crisp. Transfer to a plate, cover to keep warm. Repeat with remaining quesadillas.

4 Cut quesadillas in halves or quarters; serve with lime wedges, topped with micro coriander leaves, if you like.

Crunchy curry salad cup

 10 mins

 food swaps

Use chopped mint instead of coriander, if you prefer.

125g (4oz) cherry tomatoes
½ lebanese cucumber (65g)
½ shallot
¼ cup (70g) coconut yoghurt
1 tablespoon mango chutney
½ teaspoon curry powder
½ cup (95g) drained canned chickpeas (garbanzo beans)
2 tablespoons finely chopped coriander (cilantro)
¼ cup (6g) puffed brown rice
2 tablespoons roasted unsalted peanuts
1 tablespoon dried sweetened cranberries
1 wedge lime
2 mini pappadums (5g), to serve (optional)

1 Cut cherry tomatoes in half. Thinly slice cucumber into julienne (matchsticks). Finely chop shallot; you will need 2 teaspoons.

2 Spoon yoghurt and chutney into a 2 cup (500ml) jar with a lid (or small takeaway bowl with lid) and sprinkle over curry powder.

3 Layer chickpeas, tomato, cucumber, shallot and coriander on yoghurt mixture in the jar. Season with salt and pepper. Top with puffed rice, peanuts and cranberries (the puffed rice needs to go on top of the vegetables so it doesn't go soggy).

4 To serve, squeeze juice from lime over salad. Replace lid and shake (or toss salad in bowl). Serve with pappadums for scooping, if you like.

 **TIP**

Place 2 pappadums directly onto a microwave turntable (on opposite sides) and cook on HIGH (100%) for 45 seconds or until puffed and crisp.

Chickpea pancakes with baked beans

serves 4

30 mins

do ahead

Pancakes are best made on the day of serving.

food swaps

You can use spinach, baby spinach or silverbeet (swiss chard) in place of the kale.

vegan hacks

The beans can be heated in the microwave.

1 cup (260g) hummus
2 canned chipotle chillies in adobo sauce
2 cups (300g) chickpea flour (besan)
1 teaspoon baking powder
1 teaspoon garlic powder
¼ cup (60ml) olive oil
80g (2½oz) kale leaves, sliced thinly
2 x 420g (13½oz) cans baked beans
1 tablespoon mexican spice mix or chilli powder
2 medium avocados (500g), sliced thinly
4 radishes (140g), sliced thinly
½ cup loosely packed coriander (cilantro) sprigs
lime wedges, to serve

1 Blend or process hummus and chillies until combined.

2 Whisk chickpea flour with garlic and onion powder in a medium bowl until well combined. Make a well in the centre; add 2 cups (500ml) water, whisk until mixture is smooth. Season.

3 Heat 1 tablespoon of the oil in a large non-stick frying pan over medium heat; cook kale, stirring, for 2 minutes or until wilted. Remove from pan; cover to keep kale warm.

4 Heat another 2 teaspoons of the oil in same pan. Add a quarter of the pancake mixture; cook for 2 minutes each side or until light golden. Transfer to a plate; cover to keep warm. Repeat with remaining oil and mixture to make 4 pancakes in total.

5 Meanwhile, stir baked beans and spice mix in a small saucepan over low heat until hot.

6 Serve pancakes topped with hummus mixture, baked beans, avocado, kale, radish, coriander and lime wedges.

Nourishing rainbow bean bowl

⏳ **15 mins**

400g (12½oz) can black beans
1 teaspoon ground cumin
1 clove garlic, crushed
2 tablespoons lime juice
2 tablespoons extra virgin olive oil
⅓ cup firmly packed coriander
  (cilantro) leaves
1 corn cob (250g), husks and silks
  removed
1 medium tomato (150g), quartered
1 medium avocado (250g), quartered
60g (2oz) red cabbage, sliced thinly
1 medium carrot (120g), julienned
4 butter lettuce leaves
vegan mayonnaise, to serve

1 Drain beans, then rinse well; place in a small bowl.

2 Process cumin, garlic, lime juice, oil and coriander in a small food processor until smooth. Add dressing to beans; toss gently to combine.

3 Heat a chargrill pan (or heavy-based frying pan) over high heat. Cook corn, rotating on all sides for 8 minutes or until lightly charred. Cool slightly; cut kernels from cob.

4 Divide bean mixture, corn, tomato, avocado, cabbage, carrot and lettuce between two bowls. Top with vegan mayonnaise; season.

serves 2

Broad bean, apple & walnut open sandwich

 20 mins

 vegan hacks

Cashew spread can be found in the health food aisle of the supermarket or at health food stores.

1 cup (150g) frozen broad (fava) beans, thawed
1 teaspoon finely grated lemon rind
1 tablespoon lemon juice
1 tablespoon coarsely chopped dill
1 tablespoon coarsely chopped mint
2 trimmed celery stalks (200g), sliced thinly
½ small red apple (65g), sliced thinly
¼ cup (25g) coarsely chopped walnuts
2 thick slices multigrain sourdough bread (140g), toasted
2 tablespoons cashew nut spread
4 baby cos (romaine) lettuce leaves (20g)
micro watercress and extra grated lemon rind, to serve (optional)

1 Place broad beans in a large heatproof bowl, cover with boiling water; stand for 3 minutes. Rinse under cold water; drain, then peel.

2 Combine beans, rind, juice, dill, mint, celery, apple and walnuts in a large bowl. Season to taste.

3 Spread toasted bread slices with cashew spread. Top each with two lettuce leaves; divide the bean mixture between slices.

4 Sprinkle with watercress and extra lemon rind, if you like.

Tomato & white bean puree salad

 serves 2

80g (2½oz) ciabatta bread, torn
200g (12½oz) can cannellini beans,
 drained, rinsed (see tips)
1 clove garlic, crushed
2 teaspoons lemon juice
2 teaspoons extra virgin olive oil
200g (6½oz) medley tomatoes,
 sliced
3 teaspoons red wine vinegar
2 tablespoons small fresh
 basil leaves

1 Preheat grill (broiler) to high.
Place bread on an oven tray; grill for
1 minute or until browned lightly.

2 Blend or process beans, garlic, juice
and oil until smooth. Season to taste.

3 Combine tomatoes, vinegar and
two-thirds of the basil in a small bowl;
toss gently to combine.

4 Serve bean puree topped with
tomato salad and bread; sprinkle
with remaining basil.

25 mins

 TIP

Depending on the brand of
cannellini beans you use, you
may need to add 1 tablespoon
water to reach the desired
consistency.

Mushroom & herb salad on crunchy bread

⧗ **20 mins**

2 teaspoons extra virgin olive
400g (12½oz) mixed mushrooms,
   sliced thickly
2 teaspoons lemon thyme leaves
1 fresh small red chilli, seeded,
   chopped finely
2 cloves garlic
1 teaspoon lemon juice
1 wholemeal sourdough loaf (675g)

herb salad

½ teaspoon cumin seeds
1 teaspoon coarsely chopped
   sunflower seeds
1 teaspoon black chia seeds
2 teaspoons extra virgin olive oil
2 teaspoons lemon juice
½ small red onion (50g),
   sliced thinly
⅓ cup flat-leaf parsley leaves
⅓ cup mint leaves
1 tablespoon dill sprigs
1 tablespoon small tarragon leaves

1 Preheat grill (broiler) to high.

2 Make herb salad.

3 Heat oil in a large non-stick frying pan over high heat; cook mushrooms, lemon thyme and chilli, stirring occasionally, for 4 minutes or until browned lightly. Add 1 clove crushed garlic; cook for 1 minute or until fragrant. Remove from heat, stir through lemon juice. Season to taste. Cover to keep warm.

4 Cut bread 2cm (¾in) from the base lengthways (save the upper portion for another use). Place bread base on a large oven tray; grill for 1 minute or until toasted lightly. Halve remaining garlic clove crossways, rub warm bread with cut garlic.

5 Top bread with mushroom mixture, any pan juices and herb salad. Cut in half to serve.

herb salad

Heat a large non-stick frying pan over medium heat; cook cumin, sunflower and chia seeds, stirring, for 2 minutes or until seeds are toasted. Transfer to a small bowl. Add remaining ingredients; toss to combine.

Kale, orange & toasted mixed seed salad

serves 4

 20 mins

 do ahead

Orange and tahini dressing can be made 2 hours ahead but will thicken on standing; whisk in a little extra cold water or orange juice before serving.

1 medium blood orange (240g)
¼ cup (70g) hulled tahini
2 tablespoons sunflower seeds
2 tablespoons pepitas (pumpkin seed kernels)
1 tablespoon black sesame seeds
250g (8oz) kale
1 tablespoon olive oil
400g (12½oz) can chickpeas (garbanzo beans), drained, rinsed

1 Finely grate rind from orange; reserve 1 teaspoon for the dressing. Segment orange by peeling rind thickly from orange so no white pith remains. Cut between membranes, over a bowl to catch juice, releasing segments into another bowl. Squeeze juice from membranes; you will need 2 tablespoons juice for the dressing.

2 For dressing, whisk tahini with reserved rind and juice in a small bowl. Gradually add enough of ¼ cup (60ml) warm water until dressing becomes a pouring consistency; whisk until smooth. Season to taste.

3 Place seeds in a small frying pan; stir seeds continuously over medium heat for 2 minutes or until they are lightly browned. Transfer to a small bowl.

4 Remove stems from kale. Place kale in a large bowl with oil; rub oil into kale until leaves begin to soften.

5 Add chickpeas, orange segments and dressing to kale; toss gently to combine. Serve salad sprinkled with toasted seeds. Season.

serves 4

Polenta-crusted okra, asparagus & zucchini

 30 mins

 food swaps

Use white or red wine vinegar instead of sherry vinegar. Use vegan aïoli instead of mayonnaise; you can find it in the condiments section of some major supermarkets.

⅓ cup (55g) instant polenta (cornmeal)
1 cup (135g) gluten-free self-raising flour
1 teaspoon fine sea salt
1½ cups (375ml) chilled soda water
8 zucchini flowers, with small zucchini attached
2 tablespoons cashew cheese, crumbled
1 bunch thick-stemmed asparagus (170g)
200g (6½oz) okra
3 cups (750ml) vegetable oil
vegan mayonnaise, to serve

green capsicum salsa
½ small red onion (50g)
1 small green capsicum (bell pepper) (150g)
1 tablespoon fresh oregano leaves
2 tablespoons sherry vinegar
pinch cayenne pepper
⅓ cup (80ml) extra virgin olive oil

1 Make green capsicum salsa.

2 To make batter, combine polenta, flour and salt in a medium bowl; gradually whisk in soda water to form a thin batter.

3 Gently untwist zucchini flowers and remove the yellow stamen in the centre. Fill with 1 teaspoon of cashew cheese; re-cover with petals. Trim woody ends from asparagus and tops from okra.

4 Heat oil in a medium, deep frying pan over medium heat. Drop a tiny bit of batter into oil; if the batter sizzles the oil is ready. Dip zucchini flowers, asparagus and okra into batter, in batches, allowing excess to drain off. Shallow-fry for 1 minute or until pale golden. Drain on paper towel; season with salt flakes.

5 Serve polenta-crusted vegetables immediately with green capsicum salsa and vegan mayonnaise.

green capsicum salsa
Finely chop onion, capsicum and oregano. Place onion and vinegar in a small bowl; stand for 10 minutes. Stir in remaining ingredients; season.

Dinners

Spicy bean quesadillas

serves 2

4 flour tortillas (160g)

¾ cup (180g) refried black beans (see food swaps)

100g (3oz) firm tofu, chopped finely

100g (3oz) chopped drained roasted red capsicums (bell peppers)

1 small zucchini (90g), peeled into ribbons

2 tablespoons pickled jalapeño chillies

olive oil cooking spray

1 medium avocado (250g), sliced

mexican hot sauce, coriander leaves and lime wedges, to serve

1 Place tortillas on a work bench; spread with refried beans. Top two tortillas with tofu, capsicum, zucchini and jalapeños. Top with remaining tortillas, bean-side down; press to seal slightly.

2 Heat a large frying pan or grill plate over medium-high heat; spray with oil. Cook quesadillas, one at a time, for 2 minutes each side or until golden and crisp.

3 Cut quesadillas into wedges; top with avocado. Serve with hot sauce, coriander and lime wedges.

 15 mins

 food swaps

Use refried kidney beans instead of the black beans if they are not available or simply to try a different flavour.

vegan hacks

If you have one, you can cook the quesadillas in a baking-paper-lined sandwich press for 4 minutes each.

serves 6

Pea & coconut soup

⏳ **15 mins**

2 tablespoons coconut oil
200g (6½oz) green onions
    (scallions), sliced
1kg (2lb) frozen peas
400ml can coconut cream
3 teaspoons sea salt flakes,
    or to taste
⅓ cup (80ml) lemon juice
2 cups basil leaves
2 cups coriander (cilantro) leaves
½ cup dill sprigs
½ cup mint sprigs
unsweetened coconut yoghurt,
    to serve (optional)

1 Heat coconut oil in a large saucepan over medium-high heat. Cook green onion, stirring for 3 minutes or until softened. Increase heat to high; add peas, coconut cream, salt and 3 cups (750ml) boiling water. Bring mixture to the boil; cook, stirring occasionally, for 5 minutes or until the peas are heated through.

2 Remove from heat, add lemon juice and all but ½ cup of the combined herbs. Cool for 5 minutes; process in batches until just smooth. Return soup to pan; heat briefly until just warmed through.

3 Serve soup in bowls topped with remaining herbs and yoghurt, if you like. Season to taste.

Sweet & spicy tofu noodles

serves
2

200g (6½oz) dried rice stick noodles
250g (8oz) firm tofu
1 tablespoon peanut oil
1 clove garlic, crushed
1 tablespoon finely chopped
  fresh ginger
250g (8oz) packet fresh stir-fry
  vegetables
¼ cup (60ml) sweet chilli sauce
2 tablespoons sriracha
2 teaspoons tamari
50g (1½oz) bean sprouts, plus extra
  to serve
2 tablespoons fried shallots
⅓ cup coriander (cilantro) leaves

1 Place noodles in a large heatproof bowl; pour over enough boiling water to cover. Stand for 5 minutes or until noodles soften. Drain.

2 Meanwhile, pat tofu dry with paper towel to remove as much moisture as possible. Cut tofu into 2cm (¾in) cubes.

3 Heat oil in a wok or large frying pan over medium-high heat. Add tofu; cook for 1 minute each side or until golden. Remove with a slotted spoon. Add garlic, ginger and stir-fry vegetables to wok; cook for 1 minute or until vegetables are just starting to soften.

4 Add noodles, combined sauces and bean sprouts; stir-fry gently to prevent noodles breaking up, until combined and heated through.

5 Divide mixture between bowls. Top with tofu, extra bean sprouts, fried shallots and coriander.

 25 mins

 serving ideas

You could also serve the stir-fry topped with sliced chilli, chopped peanuts and lime wedges.

Sweet potatoes with chickpea tabbouleh

serves 4

 20 mins

 food swaps

You can use kidney or black beans instead of chickpeas.

4 small orange sweet potatoes (1kg) (see tips)

400g (12½oz) can chickpeas (garbanzo beans), drained, rinsed, chopped coarsely

2 small tomatoes (180g), chopped finely

1 lebanese cucumber (130g), chopped finely

2 green onions (scallion), chopped finely

½ cup small mint leaves (see tips)

½ cup (130g) hummus

2 tablespoons lemon juice

1 tablespoon extra virgin olive oil

¼ teaspoon sumac

1 Pierce the sweet potatoes a few times with a sharp knife. Microwave on HIGH (100%) for 8 minutes or until soft.

2 Meanwhile, combine chickpeas, tomato, cucumber, green onion and mint in a medium bowl; season.

3 Whisk hummus, lemon juice and 2 tablespoons water in a small bowl until smooth; season to taste.

4 Cut sweet potatoes lengthways along the top, being careful not to cut all the way through. Squeeze the sides gently to create a well in the centre. Fill potatoes with chickpea tabbouleh; drizzle with hummus dressing and olive oil, then sprinkle with sumac.

TIPS

Try to buy sweet potatoes that are equal in size so they cook evenly in the microwave. We used mint in this recipe; you can use any chopped soft-leaf herb such as flat-leaf parsley, dill or coriander (cilantro).

serves 4

30 mins

food swaps

Yellow patty pan squash, also known as button squash, are a summer vegetable; if unavailable substitute with yellow or grey zucchini.

¼ cup (60ml) olive oil
500g (16oz) firm tofu, cubed
250g (8oz) yellow patty pan squash, halved crossways
350g (11oz) zucchini, halved lengthways, chopped coarsely
2 teaspoons finely grated fresh ginger
2 cloves garlic, crushed
1 tablespoon light soy sauce
180g (5½oz) dried soba noodles
½ cup (75g) roasted cashews, chopped coarsely
1 cup coriander (cilantro) leaves

coriander pesto

1 cup (150g) roasted cashews
3 cups coriander (cilantro) leaves
1 clove garlic, crushed
2 teaspoons finely grated lemon rind
1 tablespoon lemon juice
1 fresh long green chilli, seeded, chopped coarsely
½ cup (125ml) olive oil

1 Make coriander pesto.

2 Heat 2 tablespoons of the oil in a large deep frying pan over high heat; cook tofu for 3 minutes each side or until golden. Remove from pan; cover to keep warm.

3 Heat remaining oil in same pan; cook squash and zucchini, stirring for 5 minutes or until golden and tender. Add ginger and garlic; cook, stirring for 30 seconds or until fragrant. Add sauce; cook for 1 minute.

4 Meanwhile, cook noodles in a large saucepan of boiling water until just tender; drain. Return noodles to pan, add pesto; toss to combine.

5 Serve noodles with zucchini mixture and tofu; top with chopped cashews and coriander.

coriander pesto

Blend or process ingredients until smooth; season to taste.

TIPS

You will need to buy 3 bunches of coriander (cilantro) for this recipe. Make extra pesto, and keep refrigerated, to mix with pasta for a quick dinner.

Mushroom, spinach & walnut pasta

serves 2

 20 mins

vegan hacks

Spelt is an ancient grain with similarities to wheat. Unlike plain flour, which is refined by removing the germ and the bran, the nutritious part of the spelt grain remains when it's milled into wholemeal flour.

⅓ cup (80ml) extra virgin olive oil
½ cup (50g) walnuts
125g (4oz) spelt spirals (see tip)
150g (4½oz) asian mixed mushrooms, sliced
2 cloves garlic, chopped finely
1 fresh long red chilli, seeded, chopped finely
2 teaspoons apple cider vinegar
280g (9oz) baby spinach leaves, washed

1 Heat 1 tablespoon olive oil in a small frying pan over medium heat; cook walnuts, stirring continuously, for 5 minutes or until golden and toasted. Remove from pan; cool. Chop nuts coarsely.

2 Cook pasta in a large saucepan of boiling salted water for 12 minutes or until almost tender. Drain. Return pasta to pan off the heat; cover and keep warm.

3 Meanwhile, heat remaining olive oil in a medium saucepan over medium-high heat; cook mushrooms for 2 minutes or until tender and golden. Add garlic and chilli; cook, stirring for 1 minute or until fragrant. Add vinegar; cook for 1 minute. Add spinach and toasted walnuts; cook for 1 minute or until spinach is lightly wilted. Season.

4 Add mushroom mixture to pasta; toss well to coat pasta. Serve.

TIP You can find spelt pasta at health food shops and most major supermarkets. You can use any shaped spelt pasta for this recipe.

Polenta with rainbow chard & chilli beans

serves 2

20 mins

food swaps

Use regular silverbeet instead of rainbow chard.

vegan hacks

Rainbow chard is silverbeet with brightly coloured yellow, orange and red stalks. Eating plant foods like chard with vitamin C-rich foods like citrus will increase your uptake of iron from the chard.

1 bunch rainbow chard (750g), trimmed (see food swaps)
2 vegan vegetable stock cubes
¼ cup (60ml) extra virgin olive oil
2 cloves garlic, sliced
400g (12½oz) can cannellini beans, drained, rinsed
¾ teaspoon dried chilli flakes
¾ cup (130g) instant polenta (cornmeal)
lemon cheeks, to serve

1 Tear leaves from chard stalks. Using a vegetable peeler, peel stalks into thin ribbons. Place ribbons in a bowl of iced water for 5 minutes or until curled.

2 Place 1 litre (4 cups) water in a medium saucepan with crumbled stock cubes; bring to a simmer over medium-high heat.

3 Meanwhile, heat 2 tablespoons of the olive oil in a large frying pan over medium-high heat. Add garlic; cook for a few minutes or until golden. Remove with a slotted spoon; reserve for serving. Add beans and chilli flakes to pan; cook, stirring, for 5 minutes or until bean skins are crisp. Remove with a slotted spoon.

4 Heat remaining oil in same pan; cook chard stems, stirring for 3 minutes or until tender and crisp. Add chard leaves and 2 tablespoons water; cook, covered, for 2 minutes or until leaves just wilt. Season to taste.

5 Slowly add polenta to simmering stock in a thin steady stream, whisking continuously. Reduce heat to low-medium; continue whisking for 2 minutes or until polenta boils and thickens. Remove from heat; stir with a wooden spoon for 1 minute. Season to taste.

6 Ladle soft polenta over a platter, top with chard mixture and crisp beans; sprinkle with fried garlic. Drizzle with a little extra olive oil, if you like. Serve immediately (polenta will thicken on standing), with lemon cheeks.

**serves
4**

Sweet potato & chickpea curry

 **30
mins**

 **vegan
hacks**

When buying the
curry paste, check
the label to ensure it
doesn't contain any
animal products.

 **serving
idea**

Serve with steamed
brown or white rice.

2 tablespoons vegetable oil
2 cloves garlic, chopped
1 tablespoon finely grated
   fresh ginger
¼ cup (75g) thai red curry paste
   (see vegan hacks)
1 medium orange sweet potato
   (400g), grated coarsely
270ml can coconut milk
2 cups (500ml) vegetable stock
200g (6½oz) firm tofu, diced
400g (12½oz) can chickpeas
   (garbanzo beans), drained, rinsed
100g (3oz) broccoli, cut into florets
1 medium red capsicum (bell
   pepper) (200g), chopped coarsely
120g (4oz) green beans, halved
⅓ cup coriander (cilantro) leaves
lime cheeks, to serve

1 Heat oil in a large saucepan over
low heat; cook garlic, ginger, curry
paste and sweet potato, stirring, for
5 minutes or until sweet potato is
tender. Stir in coconut milk and stock.
Remove pan from heat. Using a stick
blender; blend until almost smooth.

2 Return pan to heat; bring to a
simmer. Add tofu, chickpeas and
vegetables; simmer for 5 minutes or
until vegetables are just tender.
Season to taste.

3 Serve curry topped with coriander;
accompany with lime cheeks.

TIP

**If you don't have a stick
blender; cool the mixture
slightly, then process or
blend in batches, to avoid the
steam blowing the lid off.**

serves 2

Cauli steaks with almonds & tahini

30 mins

food swaps

You can use raisins or chopped dried figs instead of pomegranate seeds.

vegan hacks

Loose ready-to-use pomegranate seeds (arils) can be found in the fresh food section of supermarkets.

serving ideas

Sprinkle with grated lemon rind and serve with lemon wedges.

1 medium cauliflower (1.5kg)
¼ cup (60ml) extra virgin olive oil
2 teaspoons cumin seeds
⅓ cup (30g) natural sliced almonds
2 tablespoons tahini
2 tablespoons lemon juice
2 tablespoons pomegranate seeds (see tip)
2 tablespoons mint leaves

1 Preheat oven to 200°C/400°F.

2 Cut cauliflower into four 2cm (¾in) thick slices, leaving base and outer leaves intact. Place cauliflower steaks and any off-cuts on an oiled oven tray. Brush with 2 tablespoons of the olive oil and sprinkle with the cumin seeds.

3 Bake cauliflower for 20 minutes or until golden and tender. Turn steaks over, scatter with almonds; bake for a further 5 minutes or until tender.

4 Meanwhile, combine tahini, juice, remaining olive oil and 2 tablespoons water until well combined. Season.

5 Place cauli steaks on a platter, drizzle with tahini sauce. Top with pomegranate seeds and mint leaves.

TIP

To remove the seeds from a fresh pomegranate, cut in half crossways. Hold the cut half, cut-side down over a bowl and hit the side of the pomegranate with a wooden spoon until all the seeds fall out.

makes 2

Mushroom 'steak' sandwiches

20 mins

vegan hacks

Mushrooms have a savoury umami quality and a dense texture much like meat. They have a low calorific density and contain an important mix of minerals and vitamins. Mushrooms are also one of the leading plant-based sources for selenium, an antioxidant that assists in warding off chronic diseases.

¼ cup (60ml) olive oil
1 large onion (200g), sliced thinly
1 large green capsicum (bell pepper) (350g), sliced thinly
375g (12oz) portobello mushrooms, sliced
2 cloves garlic, crushed
2 tablespoons smoky barbecue sauce
⅓ cup (80ml) vegan beef-like stock (see tip)
2 slices vegan cheddar (36g), halved
2 long seeded bread rolls (100g), split in half
2 tablespoons american mustard
fresh or pickled sliced jalapeño chillies, to serve (optional)

1 Heat olive oil in a large non-stick frying pan over high heat; cook onion and capsicum for 4 minutes or until softened. Add mushrooms; cook stirring, for 5 minutes or until golden. Add garlic; stir for 1 minute. Add barbecue sauce and stock; cook for 2 minutes or until thickened. Season.

2 Place vegan cheddar in rolls, spoon hot mushroom mixture on top. Drizzle with mustard; top with jalapeños.

TIP

There are now an assortment of vegan stocks in the market place that mimic chicken and beef flavours, these are labelled beef or chicken 'style' or 'like' and contain no animal products.

serves 4

Greens galore couscous salad

 30 mins

 food swaps

You could also use wholemeal pearl couscous for this recipe, available from some delis; follow cooking directions on packet.

1 cup (200g) wholemeal couscous
150g (4½oz) fresh podded peas (see tip)
200g (7oz) sugar snap peas, halved lengthways
3 green onions (scallions), sliced thinly
1 small green capsicum (bell pepper) (150g), sliced thinly
2 medium avocados (500g), sliced thinly
⅓ cup (45g) chopped pistachios
¼ cup dill sprigs
¼ cup coriander (cilantro) leaves
¼ cup mint leaves
¼ cup (60ml) lime juice
⅓ cup (80ml) olive oil
1 clove garlic, crushed
lime wedges, to serve

1 Place couscous and 1 cup (250ml) boiling water in a large heatproof bowl. Cover; stand for 5 minutes or until liquid is absorbed, fluffing with a fork occasionally.

2 Meanwhile, place peas and sugar snap peas in a medium heatproof bowl; add enough boiling water to cover. Stand for 1 minute, drain. Refresh in another bowl of iced water; drain.

3 Add peas to couscous with green onion, capsicum, avocado, half the pistachios and herbs in a large bowl.

4 Place juice, oil and garlic in a screw-top jar; shake well. Season to taste.

5 Add dressing to salad. Serve salad topped with remaining pistachios and lime wedges.

TIP Podded fresh peas are available from some greengrocers. If unavailable, you will need to buy about 300g (9½oz) peas in the pod.

Popcorn cauliflower

 25 mins

vegan hacks

Use your favourite relish to dip the popcorn cauliflower into; check the jar label to ensure the brand is vegan.

2 tablespoons linseed meal (flaxmeal)
¼ cup (70g) dijon mustard
2 tablespoons hot sauce (see tips)
1⅔ cups (250g) plain (all-purpose) flour
2 teaspoons onion powder
2 teaspoons garlic powder
2 teaspoons smoked paprika
½ teaspoon cayenne pepper
½ teaspoon ground white pepper
1 medium cauliflower (1.5kg)
vegetable oil, to deep-fry
spicy tomato relish, to serve (see vegan hacks)
lemon wedges, to serve

1 Combine linseed meal with ⅔ cup (160ml) water in a large bowl; stand for 5 minutes or until thickened. Add mustard and hot sauce; stir to combine. In a second large bowl, combine flour, onion and garlic powder, spices and white pepper; season with salt.

2 Cut whole cauliflower into 2.5cm (1in) florets.

3 Fill a large saucepan one-third full with oil; heat to 180°C/350°F (or until a cube of bread turns golden in 15 seconds). Add cauliflower to linseed mixture; stir to coat. Working in batches, toss cauliflower in flour mixture to coat. Carefully lower coated cauliflower into hot oil; fry for 2 minutes or until golden. Drain on paper towel. Season with salt.

4 Serve cauliflower with tomato relish and lemon wedges.

TIP Use whatever hot sauce you have on hand, such as sriracha or Tabasco. Serve the popcorn cauliflower in tortillas with a cabbage slaw for a delicous dinner option.

Spaghetti with garlic & oil

serves 4

15 mins

500g (1lb) spaghetti
⅓ cup (80ml) extra virgin olive oil
3 cloves garlic, sliced thinly
2 tablespoons finely chopped
   flat-leaf parsley

1 Cook pasta in a large saucepan of boiling salted water until almost tender; drain, reserving some of the cooking water.

2 Meanwhile, heat oil in a large frying pan over low heat; cook garlic until golden. Stir in parsley.

3 Add garlic mixture to pasta with a little reserved pasta water if needed; toss to combine.

flavour variations

fresh tomato & seeds

Halve 500g (8oz) cherry tomatoes. Process half the tomatoes with 1 finely chopped shallot and 1 tablespoon white balsamic vinegar until smooth. Stir pureed tomato mixture, remaining tomato halves and 50g (1½oz) each toasted pine nuts, pepitas (pumpkin seed kernels) and sunflower seeds into pasta to combine. Stir in 50g (1½oz) baby rocket (arugula) leaves.

mushrooms

Thickly slice 400g (12½oz) swiss brown mushrooms. Heat ⅓ cup (80ml) extra virgin olive oil in a large frying pan over medium heat; cook mushrooms, stirring occasionally, for 10 minutes or until softened and golden. Add 1 clove crushed garlic and 2 tablespoons toasted pine nuts; cook for 1 minute or until fragrant. Season. Stir into pasta to combine.

makes
10

Vegetable spring rolls

 25 mins

 serving ideas

Serve spring rolls with a sweet chilli sauce or sriracha for an extra chilli kick. Accompany with steamed asian greens and white or brown rice for a substantial dinner option.

50g (1½oz) dried rice vermicelli noodles
1 tablespoon peanut oil
1 clove garlic, crushed
2 tablespoons finely chopped fresh ginger
1 shallot, sliced thinly
1 large carrot (180g), cut into matchsticks
½ teaspoon chinese five-spice powder
2 cups (160g) shredded wombok (napa cabbage)
1 teaspoon sesame oil
2 tablespoons tamari
1 teaspoon cornflour (cornstarch)
10 x 20cm (8in) frozen spring roll wrappers (see tip)
3 cups (750ml) vegetable oil

1 Place vermicelli in a medium heatproof bowl; pour over enough boiling water to cover. Stand for 2 minutes or until soft; drain well. Using scissors, snip noodles into shorter length.

2 Heat oil in a large wok or frying pan over medium-high heat. Add garlic, ginger, shallot and carrot; stir-fry for 5 minutes or until carrot is soft. Stir in five-spice, wombok and sesame oil; stir-fry for 1 minute.

3 Combine tamari and cornflour in a small bowl. Add to vegetables, stir until thickened slightly. Transfer mixture to bowl, stir in vermicelli until combined. Cool to room temperature.

4 Place a spring roll wrapper on flat surface. Place ¼ cup of filling, one-third up from the bottom edge in a line, leaving 1.5cm (¾in) border at each side. Fold over once, then fold in the sides and roll up to enclose filling; brush the join with a little water to seal. Repeat with remaining wrappers and filling.

5 Heat oil in a medium saucepan over medium heat until 190°C/375°F (or until a small cube of bread browns in 10 seconds). Fry spring rolls for 3 minutes or until golden and crisp. Drain on paper towel over a wire rack.

TIP You will find spring roll wrappers in the freezer section of the supermarket. Thaw before using.

Coconut, tomato & lentil soup

30 mins

vegan hacks

Turn this soup into a curry by reducing the quantity of stock by 1 cup. You could also serve the soup topped with coarsely chopped smoked almonds or crushed pappadums.

keep it

Soup can be frozen at the end of step 2. Freeze in airtight containers for up to 1 month.

1 tablespoon coconut oil
1 small onion (80g), sliced thinly
2 teaspoons yellow mustard seeds
2 teaspoons curry powder
2 tablespoons tomato paste
1 cup (200g) red lentils
1 litre (4 cups) vegetable stock
½ cup (125ml) coconut milk,
    plus extra to drizzle
2 medium tomatoes (300g)
coriander (cilantro) leaves and
    lemon wedges, to serve

1 Heat coconut oil in a medium saucepan over medium-high heat; cook onion, stirring, for 3 minutes or until soft. Add mustard seeds; stir for 4 minutes or until they start to pop. Add curry powder; cook, stirring, for 1 minute. Add tomato paste; cook, stirring, for a further 30 seconds.

2 Add lentils, stock and coconut milk; bring to the boil. Reduce heat to low; simmer, covered, stirring occasionally for 10 minutes or until lentils are tender. Coarsely chop 1 fresh tomato; stir into soup until just heated through. Season to taste.

3 Coarsely chop remaining fresh tomato. Ladle soup into bowls; drizzle with a little extra coconut milk, then top with chopped tomato and coriander leaves. Serve soup with lemon wedges.

serves 2

Soba noodles with chilli garlic sauce

20 mins

vegan hacks

If you can find shelled edamame you will need 120g (4oz).

food swaps

Green beans, frozen peas and sugar snap peas can be used in place of the edamame.

3 green onions (scallions)
½ teaspoon dried chilli flakes
2 small cloves garlic, crushed
2 tablespoons tamari
2 tablespoons chinese black vinegar
2 tablespoons sesame oil
1 bunch choy sum (500g), trimmed, halved
180g (5½oz) dried green tea soba noodles
250g (8oz) frozen edamame (soybeans), thawed, shelled
toasted sesame seeds, to serve (optional)

1 Cut 1 green onion into 6cm (2½in) lengths, then into long strips; place in a bowl of iced water to curl. Thinly slice remaining green onions.

2 Combine chilli flakes, garlic, tamari, vinegar, 1 tablespoon sesame oil and the sliced green onion in a small bowl.

3 Bring a saucepan of salted water to the boil over high heat. Cook choy sum for 1 minute or until tender and crisp. Remove with tongs; place on a plate and drizzle with remaining 1 tablespoon sesame oil.

4 Return the saucepan of water to the boil. Add noodles; cook for 3 minutes. Add edamame to noodles; cook for a further 1 minute or until noodles are tender and edamame heated through. Drain; return noodles and edamame to pan. Add chilli garlic sauce; toss gently to combine.

5 Divide noodle mixture and choy sum between bowls; top with green onion curls and sesame seeds.

serves 4

Smoky sweet corn chowder

 30 mins

 vegan hacks

Any leftover or unused cauliflower can be used to make Cauliflower couscous on page 173.

3 green onions (scallions)
½ small cauliflower (500g), trimmed, chopped finely
1kg (2lb) frozen corn kernels, thawed
2 cups (500ml) vegetable stock
½ teaspoon garlic powder
½ teaspoon ground turmeric
400ml can coconut milk
3 cups (45g) salted natural popcorn
1 tablespoon smoked paprika
1 tablespoon extra virgin olive oil

1 Thinly slice green onions; reserve dark green tips. Place white and light green part of onions in a large saucepan with cauliflower, corn kernels, stock, garlic powder and turmeric. Cover with a tight-fitting lid; bring to the boil. Reduce heat to medium; simmer for 20 minutes or until vegetables are tender.

2 Remove pan from heat. Using a stick blender, blend stock and vegetables until almost smooth. Return pan to medium heat; stir in coconut milk, then bring to a simmer. Season.

3 Meanwhile, place popcorn and smoked paprika in a large bowl; toss until well coated.

4 Ladle soup into bowls; drizzle with oil. Top with seasoned popcorn and reserved shredded green onion tips.

TIPS

To chop cauliflower you can pulse it in food processor. To thaw corn quickly, place in a colander and pour over boiling water. If you don't have a stick blender; cool the mixture, then process or blend in batches.

serves 2

Fried rice

Don't miss your fave takeaway with these easy vegan recipes

Fried rice is the perfect way to use up leftover rice, as day-old rice becomes crisper when stir-fried. Use whatever type of rice you have on hand.

Extra veg fried rice

prep + cook time 20 minutes

From 1 bunch gai lan, coarsely chop leaves and stems, keeping each part separate. Drain and pat dry 200g (6½oz) silken tofu, then slice. Heat 2 teaspoons each vegetable and sesame oil in a wok; stir-fry tofu for 3 minutes or until crisp and broken up. Remove from wok. Stir-fry 1 finely chopped onion, carrot, capsicum (bell pepper) and 10 snow peas for 2 minutes or until softened. Add gai lan stalks; stir-fry for a further 2 minutes. Remove from wok. Heat 1 tablespoon vegetable oil and 2 teaspoons sesame oil in wok. Add 250g (4oz) packet microwave brown rice and 1 teaspoon chinese five-spice powder; stir-fry for 3 minutes or until heated through. Stir in vegetables, gai lan leaves, tofu and 2 tablespoons tamari. Serve fried rice with sriracha.

Chicken-like fried rice

prep + cook time 20 minutes

Split 1 bunch broccolini in half lengthways. Cut a 200g (6½oz) block tempeh into small cubes. Combine 2 tablespoons each tamari, rice wine vinegar and sriracha in a small bowl. Heat 1 tablespoon vegetable oil in a wok over medium heat; stir-fry tempeh for 5 minutes or until golden on all sides. Remove from wok; keep warm. Add 250g (4oz) microwave long-grain white rice; stir-fry until heated through. Remove from wok; keep warm. Add broccolini and ½ cup frozen peas to wok; stir-fry until bright green. Return rice to wok with tamari mixture, toss to combine. Serve fried rice topped with tempeh, sliced long red chilli and lime wedges.

Kimchi fried rice

prep + cook time 15 minutes

Thinly slice 6 green onions, keeping white part and green part separate. Reserve a small handful of green onion to serve. Heat 2 tablespoons vegetable oil and 3 teaspoons sesame oil in a wok over medium-high heat. Stir-fry white part of onion and 2 teaspoons gochungung (korean red pepper paste) for 1 minute. Add 2 x 250g (4oz) packets microwave short-grain rice; stir-fry for 5 minutes or until heated through. Add 1 cup chopped kimchi, ½ cup shelled thawed edamame (soybeans) and green part of onions; stir-fry until heated through. Serve fried rice topped with reserved green onion, a handful of bean sprouts and purchased toasted sesame nori crisps.

Tom yum fried rice

prep + cook time 20 minutes

Trim 400g (12½oz) green beans; halve lengthways. Wash 1 bunch coriander (cilantro), paying attention to roots. Pick leaves from coriander; you need 1 cup. Coarsely chop coriander stems and roots; you need ½ cup. Heat 2 tablespoons vegetable oil in a wok over high heat; fry 200g (6½oz) sliced firm tofu for 2 minutes on each side or until golden. Remove from wok; keep warm. Stir-fry ¼ cup vegan tom yum paste and coriander stem and root mix for 3 minutes or until fragrant. Add beans, 125g (4oz) halved cherry tomatoes and 2 x 250g (4oz) packets microwave jasmine rice; stir-fry for 3 minutes or until rice is heated through and beans are tender. Serve fried rice topped with tofu, reserved coriander leaves and lime cheeks.

serves 4

Eggplant hotdog with sauerkraut

25 mins

2 tablespoons dijon mustard
2 tablespoons pure maple syrup
1 teaspoon cumin seeds, toasted, ground (see tip)
1 teaspoon sea salt flakes
4 medium lebanese eggplant (240g)
4 long crusty bread rolls (320)
½ cup (130g) hummus
130g (4oz) red cabbage sauerkraut
small mint leaves and extra dijon mustard, to serve (optional)

1 Preheat a chargrill plate (or barbecue) over high heat.

2 Combine mustard, maple syrup, cumin and salt in a small bowl.

3 Cut a deep, long slit along the top of each eggplant, cutting three-quarters of the way down but not all the way through. Brush mustard mixture lightly all over eggplant, including the cut surfaces.

4 Reduce grill plate heat to medium; place eggplants on grill plate, cover with a medium heatproof bowl or foil. Cook, turning occasionally, brushing with remaining mustard mixture at each turn for 15 minutes or until eggplants are soft in the centre.

5 Cut a slit along the top of each bread roll. Divide hummus among rolls, top with eggplant, sauerkraut, mint leaves and extra mustard.

TIP

Toasting and grinding whole spices amplifies and freshens the flavour. Place cumin seeds in a frying pan; stir until fragrant. Grind using a mortar and pestle. Alternatively, you can use 1 teaspoon ground cumin.

Tandoori tofu kebabs with mint yoghurt

30 mins

vegan hacks

Check the back label of the coconut yoghurt as sugar is not always declared on the front label.

serving ideas

Serve kebabs with warm naan bread or steamed jasmine rice.

500g (1lb) firm tofu
1 medium red capsicum (bell pepper) (200g)
1 medium red onion (170g)
2 medium tomatoes (300g)
2 tablespoons tandoori paste
⅓ cup (95g) coconut yoghurt
1 tablespoon small mint leaves
lime wedges, to serve

mint yoghurt
½ cup (140g) coconut yoghurt
2 tablespoons finely chopped mint leaves
¼ cup (60ml) fresh lime juice

1 Preheat an oiled barbecue flat plate. Soak four bamboo skewers in cold water to prevent them scorching.

2 Meanwhile, pat tofu dry with paper towel to remove as much moisture as possible, then cut into 2cm x 4cm (¾in x 1½in) pieces. Remove seeds from capsicum. Cut capsicum and red onion into eight 4cm (1½in) pieces. Cut tomatoes into quarters.

3 Combine tandoori paste and coconut yoghurt in a medium bowl. Add tofu; stir gently until evenly coated.

4 Thread vegetables and marinated tofu, alternating, onto skewers. Cook, kebabs, for 5 minutes each side or until the vegetables are tender and tofu is golden.

5 Meanwhile, make mint yoghurt.

6 Scatter mint over kebabs; serve with mint yoghurt and lime wedges.

mint yoghurt
Process ingredients in a small food processor until smooth. (Alternatively, mix ingredients together in a small bowl.) (Makes ½ cup.)

TIPS You may want to adjust the quantity of tandoori paste if you prefer less spicy. You can also cook kebabs in a 220°C/425°F oven for 30 minutes, turning over halfway through the cooking time, or until browned.

Spicy nachos

serves 2

30 mins

food swaps

You could make the nachos with purple hued beetroot corn chips and kidney beans if you like.

125g (4oz) corn chips
½ cup (60g) vegan cheddar
¼ teaspoon cumin seeds
2 teaspoons olive oil
1 small red onion (100g), chopped finely
1 clove garlic, crushed
2 teaspoons Tabasco
2 tablespoons tomato paste
400g (12½oz) can black beans, drained, rinsed
1 medium tomato (150g), chopped finely
1 fresh long red chilli, sliced thinly
1 cup coriander (cilantro) leaves
1 tablespoon fresh lime juice
1 medium avocado (250g), sliced
lime wedges, to serve

1 Preheat oven to 180°C/350°F. Line an oven tray with baking paper.

2 Place corn chips on oven tray, arranging them towards the outer edge; scatter over vegan cheddar. Bake for 8 minutes or until cheese melts and chips are heated through.

3 Meanwhile, heat a medium frying pan over medium heat, add cumin seeds, stir for 2 minutes or until fragrant. Add olive oil, onion and garlic; cook, stirring, for 5 minutes or until onion is soft. Add Tabasco and tomato paste; cook, stirring for 1 minute. Add beans and ⅓ cup (80ml) water; cook, stirring for 2 minutes or until thickened slightly. Lightly mash some of the beans in the pan with a fork or potato masher.

4 Combine tomato, chilli, coriander and lime juice in a small bowl. Season.

5 Spoon bean mixture over the corn chips. Top with avocado slices and tomato salsa, serve with lime wedges.

serves 2

Pumpkin tabbouleh

⧗ **30 mins**

200g (6½oz) butternut pumpkin, peeled, chopped coarsely
½ small red onion (50g), cut into thin wedges
1 teaspoon olive oil
⅓ cup burghul
½ cup coarsely chopped flat-leaf parsley
180g (5½oz) cherry tomatoes, halved
2 tablespoons lemon juice
1 clove garlic, crushed

1 Preheat oven to 220°C/425°F. Line an oven tray with baking paper.

2 Combine pumpkin and onion on tray; drizzle with oil. Roast for 20 minutes or until tender. Cool; transfer to a large bowl.

3 Meanwhile, bring 1 cup (250ml) water to the boil in a small saucepan. Add burghul, reduce heat to low; cook, covered, for 15 minutes or until tender. Remove from heat; stand for 10 minutes.

4 Transfer burghul to the bowl with vegetables; mix gently to combine. Add parsley and tomatoes to pumpkin mixture. Combine juice and garlic in a small bowl, drizzle over tabbouleh; toss gently to combine.

Tofu larb with crisp rice papers

 30 mins

 vegan hacks

To press tofu dry, place the block of tofu on a paper-towel-lined plate; cover with another sheet of paper towel. Weigh down with another plate or chopping board.

250g (8oz) firm tofu
4 green onions (scallions)
⅓ cup (80ml) lime juice
¼ cup (60ml) vegetable stock
2 tablespoons soy sauce
1½ tablespoons brown sugar
2 tablespoons vegetable oil
1 fresh long red chilli, seeded, chopped finely
1 stalk lemongrass, white part only, sliced thinly
1 tablespoon finely chopped fresh ginger
1 cup (100g) coarsely chopped roasted walnuts
2 tablespoons finely chopped coriander (cilantro)
1 gem (romaine) lettuce (180g), leaves separated
1 fresh long red chilli, sliced thinly, extra
lime wedges, to serve (optional)

crisp rice papers
⅓ cup (80ml) vegetable oil
8 x 16cm (6½in) rice paper rounds

1 Pat the tofu dry with paper towel (see vegan hacks). Crumble tofu into small chunks. Thinly slice white part of green onions. Shred green tops; reserve to serve.

2 Place lime juice, stock, soy sauce and sugar in a small jug; stir until sugar dissolves. Pour half the sauce mixture into a small bowl; reserve to serve.

3 Heat oil in a large wok or frying pan over high heat; stir-fry tofu for 8 minutes or until golden. Add white part of green onion, chopped chilli, lemongrass and ginger; stir-fry for 1 minute or until fragrant. Add walnuts; stir-fry for 30 seconds. Add remaining sauce mixture to wok; bring to a simmer, cook for 2 minutes or until reduced by half. Stir in coriander. Keep warm.

4 Just before serving, make crisp rice papers.

5 Serve larb with lettuce leaves, reserved sauce and crisp rice papers, topped with reserved green onion and extra sliced chilli. Serve with lime wedges.

crisp rice papers
Heat oil in a medium frying pan over medium-high heat. Cook one rice paper at a time, for 30 seconds or until puffed. Drain on paper towel.

Zucchini noodles with cashew pesto

 20 mins

🗑 **keep it**

Store leftover pesto in an airtight container in the fridge for 1 week. Spread leftover pesto on toast or seeded crackers for a delicious snack.

4 large zucchini (600g)
125g (4oz) mixed heirloom cherry tomatoes, halved
¼ cup basil leaves
1 tablespoon pine nuts
2 tablespoons nutritional yeast flakes

cashew pesto

⅔ cup (100g) raw cashews
1 cup firmly packed basil leaves
¼ cup (40g) pine nuts
¼ cup (60ml) lemon juice
½ cup (125ml) extra virgin olive oil
2 teaspoons nutritional yeast flakes
1 clove garlic, crushed

1 Make cashew pesto.

2 Using a spiraliser or julienne peeler (see tip), cut zucchini into zoodles; place in a large bowl.

3 Add pesto and cherry tomatoes to bowl; toss to combine. Top with basil leaves, pine nuts and nutritional yeast. Serve immediately.

cashew pesto

Blend or process ingredients with 1 tablespoon water until smooth. Season to taste. (Makes 1¼ cup.)

TIP A spiraliser is a kitchen gadget that cuts vegetables to resemble noodles. If you don't have one, you can use a julienne peeler or a julienne attachment on a mandoline or V-slicer.

Curried lentil & vegetable soup

serves 6

30 mins

500g (1lb) butternut pumpkin,
    peeled, chopped coarsely
1 litre (4 cups) vegetable stock
2 teaspoons olive oil
1 medium onion (170g),
    chopped finely
1 large clove garlic, crushed
1 medium carrot (120g),
    chopped coarsely
1 stalk celery (150g), trimmed,
    chopped finely
1 fresh bay leaf
3 teaspoons curry powder
1 cup (120g) frozen peas
400g (12½oz) can brown lentils,
    drained, rinsed
¼ cup (60ml) lemon juice
¼ cup coriander (cilantro) leaves

1 Place pumpkin, stock and 1 litre
(4 cups) water in a medium saucepan;
cover, bring to the boil. Reduce heat;
simmer, uncovered, for 5 minutes or
until pumpkin is nearly tender.

2 Heat oil in a large saucepan over
high heat; cook onion, garlic, carrot,
celery and bay leaf, stirring, for
3 minutes or until softened. Add
curry powder; stir until fragrant.

3 Add pumpkin mixture and peas to
pan; simmer for 10 minutes or until
vegetables are tender. Stir in lentils
and juice. Remove and discard bay leaf.

4 Ladle soup into bowls; serve topped
with coriander.

serves 4

Cauliflower & tofu red curry

 30 mins

 vegan hacks

When buying the curry paste, check the label to ensure it doesn't contain any animal products.

serving ideas

Serve curry with steamed jasmine rice.

1 tablespoon peanut oil
1 medium onion (150g), sliced thinly
400ml can coconut milk, unopened (do not shake can) (see tip)
⅓ cup (100g) thai red curry paste (see vegan hacks)
2 teaspoons soy sauce
1 tablespoon lime juice
1 tablespoon brown sugar
400g (12½oz) cauliflower, cut into florets
250g (8oz) green beans, trimmed
1 large zucchini (150g), sliced thinly diagonally
110g (3½oz) tofu puffs, halved
⅓ cup (15g) flaked coconut, toasted
⅓ cup coriander (cilantro) leaves
lime halves, to serve

1 Heat oil in a wok over medium heat; stir-fry onion, for 2 minutes or until softened.

2 Open coconut milk can carefully. Add a spoonful of the solid coconut milk from the top of the can to wok. Add curry paste; cook, stirring, for 3 minutes or until oil separates and rises to the surface. Stir in soy sauce, juice, sugar, remaining coconut milk and ¾ cup (180ml) water; bring to the boil. Reduce heat to low-medium, add cauliflower; simmer, covered, for 5 minutes. Add green beans and zucchini; simmer, partially covered, for 5 minutes or until vegetables are tender. Add tofu; stir until hot.

3 Top curry with coconut flakes and coriander; serve immediately accompanied with lime halves.

TIP We used coconut milk that hasn't been emulsified, so it separates with the solid rising to the surface. If your coconut milk is emulsified, simply cook off the curry paste in a little extra peanut oil instead.

Gai lan & mushroom stir-fry

450g (14½oz) thin udon-style
  noodles
2 tablespoons peanut oil
2 cloves garlic, crushed
1 fresh long red chilli, sliced thinly
½ teaspoon chinese five-spice
  powder
430g (14oz) gai lan
2 tablespoons vegetarian oyster
  sauce (see vegan hacks)
2 tablespoons kecap manis
½ teaspoon sesame oil
200g (6½oz) enoki mushrooms,
  trimmed
2 tablespoons fried shallots

1 Place noodles in a medium
heatproof bowl with enough boiling
water to cover; separate noodles with
a fork. Drain well.

2 Heat peanut oil in a wok over high
heat; stir-fry garlic and chilli for
1 minute or until softened. Add five-
spice and gai lan; stir-fry for 1 minute
or until tender.

3 Add combined sauces, sesame oil
and noodles; stir-fry for 1 minute or
until noodles are heated through.
Toss through mushrooms.

4 Serve topped with shallots.

 20 mins

 vegan hacks

While regular oyster
sauce is made from
oysters and their
brine, and is not
vegan, vegetarian
oyster sauce is made
from mushrooms.

serves 4

Very green vegie curry

30 mins

serving ideas

Serve curry with steamed brown rice or grilled flatbreads.

¼ cup (60ml) olive oil
1 shallot, sliced thinly
1 tablespoon finely grated fresh ginger
1½ cups (375ml) almond and coconut milk
1½ cups (375ml) vegetable stock
1 bunch broccolini (175g), sliced
1 bunch asparagus (170g), tips reserved, stems chopped finely
150g (4½oz) green beans, halved
3 cups (105g) shredded curly kale
150g (4½oz) sugar snap peas
1½ cups thai basil leaves
1½ tablespoons tamari
1 tablespoon brown sugar
toasted flaked coconut and pepitas (pumpkin seed kernels), to serve (optional)

curry paste

3 green onions (scallions)
2 fresh long green chillies, seeded
1 stalk lemongrass
½ bunch coriander (cilantro)
½ teaspoon coriander seeds
½ teaspoon cumin seeds
2 tablespoons olive oil
4 cloves garlic, crushed
½ teaspoon ground turmeric

1 Make curry paste.

2 Heat a large wok over high heat. Add oil, shallot and ginger; cook for 2 minutes or until softened. Add curry paste; cook, stirring, for a further 2 minutes or until fragrant.

3 Add almond and coconut milk and stock; bring to the boil. Add broccolini, asparagus stems and green beans; reduce heat to medium. Simmer vegetables for 3 minutes or until almost tender.

4 Add kale, sugar snap peas, reserved asparagus tips, half the thai basil, the reserved coriander leaves from the curry paste, tamari and sugar; simmer for a further 3 minutes. Top curry with remaining thai basil, coconut flakes and pepitas, if you like.

curry paste

Coarsely chop green onions, chillies, lemongrass and coriander roots and stems (reserve coriander leaves for serving). Heat a small frying pan over medium heat. Add both coriander and cumin seeds; toast for 1 minute or until fragrant. Process all ingredients in a food processor to form a smooth paste. Season to taste.

serves 4

Spaghetti lentil bolognese

 30 mins

 vegan hacks

Check the packet label to ensure the parmesan brand is vegan. You could also use grated vegan cheddar or nutritional yeast flakes instead, if you like.

2 tablespoons olive oil
1 large onion (200g), chopped finely
2 cloves garlic, crushed
2 tablespoons coarsely chopped basil
1 teaspoon dried oregano leaves
400g (12½oz) can diced tomatoes
410g (13oz) can tomato puree
400g (12½oz) can brown lentils, drained, rinsed
400g (12½oz) spaghetti
⅓ cup (25g) dairy-free shredded parmesan-style cheese (see vegan hacks)
2 tablespoons small basil leaves, extra

1 Heat oil in a large deep frying pan over medium heat; cook onion, stirring, for 5 minutes or until golden. Stir in garlic, herbs, diced tomatoes and puree; cook for 5 minutes. Add lentils, then bring to the boil; cook, covered, for 4 minutes or until sauce thickens. Season to taste.

2 Cook pasta in a large saucepan of salted boiling water following packet directions until tender; drain.

3 Divide spaghetti and lentil bolognese among plates or bowls. Serve topped with cheese and extra basil leaves; season.

serves 2

30 mins

Sweet potato & onion pizza

1 small orange sweet potato (250g), unpeeled, sliced thinly

½ small onion (40g), cut into thin wedges

1 large wholemeal pitta bread (100g)

2 tablespoons tomato pasta sauce

1½ teaspoons finely chopped rosemary

¼ cup (30g) coarsely grated vegan cheddar

20g (¾oz) baby rocket (arugula) leaves

1 Preheat oven to 220°C/425°F. Line an oven tray with baking paper.

2 Cook sweet potato and onion on a heated oiled grill plate (or grill or barbecue) until browned both sides and tender.

3 Place bread on oven tray; spread with sauce. Layer with vegetables and sprinkle with rosemary then cheese. Bake for 8 minutes or until base is crisp and cheese has melted. Serve topped with rocket.

Salt & pepper tofu with soba noodles

⏳ **20 mins**

300g (9½oz) block medium-firm tofu
180g (5½oz) soba noodles
170g (5½oz) asparagus, trimmed, halved lengthways
1 tablespoon sesame oil
1 tablespoon rice flour
1 tablespoon sesame seeds
1 teaspoon ground white pepper
½ teaspoon freshly ground black pepper
½ teaspoon sea salt
vegetable oil, for shallow-frying
⅓ cup (80ml) teriyaki sauce
1 medium lebanese cucumber (170g), sliced thinly
1 green onion (scallion), sliced thinly
½ teaspoon sesame oil, extra (optional)

1 Place tofu on a paper-towel-lined plate; cover with another sheet of paper towel. Weigh down with another heavy plate. Stand tofu for 10 minutes to drain.

2 Meanwhile, bring a medium saucepan of water to the boil; cook noodles for 1 minute. Add asparagus to noodles; cook for a further 2 minutes or until tender. Drain.

3 Place sesame oil on a small plate. Combine flour, sesame seeds, both peppers and salt in a small shallow bowl or plate. Cut tofu into 12 cubes; lightly coat each cube in sesame oil, then coat in rice flour mixture.

4 Heat 1.5cm (¾in) vegetable oil in a non-stick frying pan over medium heat. Shallow-fry tofu, in two batches, for 2 minutes each side or until golden.

5 Meanwhile, place teriyaki sauce in same cleaned medium saucepan; warm over medium heat. Return noodles to pan; stir until warmed through.

6 Divide noodle mixture between bowls. Top with cucumber, tofu, asparagus and green onion; drizzle with extra sesame oil.

serves 4

Cauliflower couscous

 30 mins

 food swaps

Use the same amount of crunchy sprout combo instead of mung bean sprouts. Use whole or chopped pistachios or another nut for the slivered pistachios.

1 small cauliflower (1kg)
1 teaspoon sea salt flakes
1 cup firmly packed mint leaves, chopped coarsely
1 cup firmly packed coriander (cilantro) leaves, chopped coarsely
1 cup firmly packed flat-leaf parsley, chopped coarsely
300g (9½oz) fresh peas, shelled
1½ cups (150g) mung bean sprouts
½ cup (90g) pitted sicilian green olives, halved
½ cup (70g) slivered pistachios
50g (1½oz) preserved lemon, pulp discarded, rind sliced thinly (see tip)
¼ cup (60ml) extra virgin olive oil
2 tablespoons lemon juice
mint leaves extra and lemon wedges, to serve

mint yoghurt sauce

½ cup (140g) coconut yoghurt
2 tablespoons finely chopped mint leaves
¼ cup (60ml) fresh lemon juice

1 Make mint yoghurt sauce.

2 Cut cauliflower into florets. Working in batches, process cauliflower and salt, until it resembles a couscous-like consistency. Transfer to a clean tea towel, doubled piece of muslin or a nut bag; squeeze all the liquid out of the cauliflower.

3 Transfer cauliflower couscous to a large bowl; fluff with a fork. Add herbs, peas, sprouts, olives, three-quarters of the pistachios and the preserved lemon rind; mix until well combined.

4 Whisk olive oil and lemon juice in a small bowl until well combined; season. Drizzle over cauliflower couscous; stir to combine. Sprinkle with remaining pistachios. Top with extra mint leaves; serve with lemon wedges and yoghurt sauce.

mint yoghurt sauce

Process ingredients in a small food processor until smooth. (Alternatively, mix ingredients together in a small bowl.) Season to taste. (Makes ½ cup.)

TIP

Preserved lemons are a North African specialty; available from delicatessens and specialty food shops. Use the rind only. Remove and discard the fleshy pulp; rinse the rind under cold water before using.

serves 4

Corn fritters & green papaya salad

30 mins

food swaps

Use brown sugar or palm sugar instead of coconut sugar. Use your favourite chilli based sauce for the dressing.

vegan hacks

When buying chilli garlic sauce, check the jar label to ensure the brand is vegan.

½ bunch fresh coriander (cilantro), stems and roots removed
500g (1lb) green papaya, peeled
¾ cup (135g) rice flour
½ teaspoon baking powder
⅔ cup (160ml) iced water
165g corn kernels
150g (4½oz) green beans, trimmed, sliced thinly
⅓ cup (80ml) vegetable oil
2 baby gem lettuce (180g), leaves separated
250g (8oz) cherry tomatoes, quartered

chilli peanut dressing
⅓ cup (45g) roasted unsalted peanuts, chopped
½ cup (125ml) chilli garlic sauce (see vegan hacks)

1 Pick half the coriander into sprigs; reserve to serve. Finely chop remaining coriander to yield ¼ cup. Finely shred papaya using a mandoline, julienne peeler or knife.

2 Make chilli peanut dressing.

3 Combine rice flour and baking powder in a large bowl. Whisk in the iced water to form a thick batter. Add corn, beans and chopped coriander to batter; mix well. Season to taste. (The mixture will look runny but binds on cooking.)

4 Heat oil in large frying pan over high heat or until a drop of batter sizzles as soon as it is added to the pan. Working in two batches of six, drop heaped tablespoons of batter into pan; cook for 3 minutes each side or until crisp and golden.

5 Meanwhile, place lettuce leaves and tomatoes on a large platter with papaya, reserved coriander sprigs and chilli peanut dressing; serve with corn fritters. To eat, scoop a little bit of everything onto a lettuce leaf.

chilli peanut dressing
Combine ingredients in a small bowl.

Snacks & sweets

Banana with cashew butter & nutty crunch

20 mins

food swaps

If you prefer you can use a commercially made cashew butter or even crunchy peanut butter.

serving ideas

You can also try the cashew butter spread on cross sections of apple, pear or persimmon.

keep it

Nut butter will keep in an airtight container for up to 1 month. In summer, it is best stored in the fridge.

2 tablespoons natural flaked almonds

2 tablespoons sunflower seeds

2 tablespoons flaked coconut

1 tablespoon white sesame seeds

½ teaspoon ground cinnamon, plus extra to serve

1½ tablespoons rice malt syrup

2 small bananas (260g), halved lengthways

2 teaspoons rice malt syrup, extra

cashew butter

2 cups (300g) raw cashews

1 Make cashew butter.

2 Place flaked almonds, sunflower seeds, coconut, sesame seeds and cinnamon in a small frying pan, stirring continuously over medium heat, for 2 minutes or until lightly browned. Add rice malt syrup; stir continuously, for 1 minute or until browned. Transfer to a small baking-paper-lined tray. Leave to cool slightly, then break into pieces.

3 Spread 1 tablespoon of cashew butter over each banana half, drizzle with extra rice malt syrup and sprinkle with toasted seed mix and extra cinnamon.

cashew butter

Process cashews, scraping down the side of the bowl regularly, for 10-15 minutes or until completely smooth (see tip). (Makes 1 cup.)

TIP Powerful food processors will take about 10 minutes to process the cashew butter, while small home-use processors may take longer. If yours is taking a long time, add 2 tablespoons hot water to loosen.

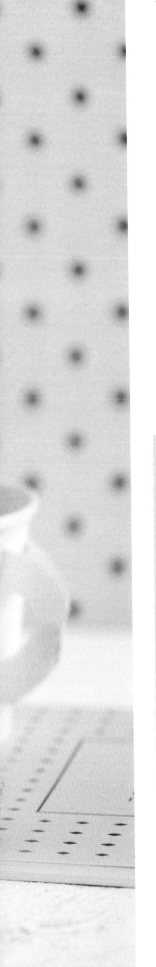

Apricot & coconut balls

 15 mins

 keep it

Store balls in an airtight container in the fridge for up to 3 weeks.

2⅔ cups (400g) dried apricots
1 cup (120g) almond meal
2 cups (160g) desiccated coconut
2 cups (300g) unsalted roasted cashews
½ cup (45g) rolled oats
2 tablespoons white chia seeds
¼ cup (70g) coconut yoghurt
1 teaspoon finely grated orange rind
1 teaspoon vanilla extract
2 tablespoons lemon juice
2 tablespoons rice bran syrup
⅓ cup (25g) desiccated coconut, extra

1 Process all ingredients, except extra coconut, until well combined and mixture clumps together and starts to clean the side of the bowl.

2 Place extra coconut in a small bowl. Shape mixture into 24 balls; roll balls in coconut to coat. Place on a tray, cover; refrigerate for 1 hour or until chilled. Transfer to an airtight container (see keep it).

Avo rainbow salad cups

1 large avocado (320g), halved
½ small carrot (35g), julienned or grated (see tip)
½ small beetroot (beet) (50g), julienned or grated (see tip)
2 tablespoons kimchi
1 tablespoon sprouts (optional)

lemon tahini dressing

1 tablespoon tahini
1 tablespoon lemon juice
2 teaspoons extra virgin olive oil

1 Make lemon tahini dressing.

2 Place avocado halves on a plate; fill each half evenly with carrot, beetroot and kimchi. Drizzle with dressing and top with sprouts; season.

lemon tahini dressing

Stir ingredients in a small bowl with 1½ tablespoons water until well combined.

 10 mins

 serving idea

For one person you can halve the recipe, or double ingredients to serve 4 (as pictured).

TIP A julienne peeler looks like a vegetable peeler with a serrated blade. They are available from kitchenware stores and Asian grocers. Alternatively, you can cut into a julienne (matchsticks), using a mandoline or sharp knife.

Super guacamole

makes 2 cups

 10 mins

 serving ideas

Arrange dip on a platter with blue corn tortillas chips and baby radishes.

1 fresh small red chilli, chopped finely
1 small clove garlic, crushed
½ teaspoon ground cumin
1 tablespoon lime juice
2 medium avocados (500g)
¼ cup finely chopped coriander (cilantro), plus extra to serve
1 teaspoon chia seeds
2 tablespoons pepitas (pumpkin seed kernels), toasted

1 Place chilli, garlic, cumin, juice, avocado flesh and coriander in a medium bowl; mash with a fork until combined.

2 Transfer dip to a serving bowl; top with chia seeds, pepitas and extra coriander leaves.

serves 8

Raw choc chip cookie dough

 15 mins

(+ refrigeration)

 keep it

Store the raw cookie dough in an airtight container, refrigerated, for up to 5 days.

100g (3oz) brazil nuts
200g (6½oz) natural almonds
½ teaspoon vanilla bean paste
¼ cup (60ml) pure maple syrup
¼ teaspoon ground cinnamon
2 tablespoons coconut oil, at room temperature
1 teaspoon sea salt flakes
¼ cup (35g) cacao nibs
vegan ice-cream and chopped vegan chocolate, to serve

1 Line an 18cm x 28cm (7¼in x 11¼in) oven tray with baking paper.

2 Process nuts until fine crumbs form. Add vanilla, maple syrup, cinnamon, coconut oil and salt; pulse until a soft dough forms (it will be quite sticky).

3 Press dough into lined oven tray, using a spoon dipped in a little cold water. Sprinkle over 2 tablespoons of the cacao nibs; press firmly into dough. Refrigerate for 25 minutes or until firm.

4 Lift baking paper and dough from tray. Using paper as an aid, roll dough into a sausage shape. Sprinkle over remaining cacao nibs, reroll in paper, then in foil. Twist ends of foil and paper to form a tight log. Refrigerate for a further 20 minutes or until firm.

5 Cut into thick slices; serve with ice-cream, topped with chocolate.

makes 16 bars

Chocolate iron power bars

20 mins

(+ refrigeration)

vegan hacks

Spirulina is available from supermarkets and health food stores. Tahini, molasses, prunes and spirulina all contain adequate amounts of iron for vegans.

keep it

Store bars in an airtight container in the fridge for up to 2 weeks or freeze for up to 1 month.

1 cup (170g) pitted prunes
¼ cup (70g) tahini
⅓ cup (75g) coconut oil, melted
2 tablespoons molasses
1½ cups (180g) almond meal
1 tablespoon cacao powder
1 teaspoon spirulina powder (optional)
2 tablespoons finely chopped pistachios

1 Grease a 12cm x 25cm (4¾in x 10in) (base measurement) loaf pan; line with baking paper.

2 Process prunes until they form a paste. Add tahini, coconut oil and molasses; process briefly until just combined. Add almond meal, cacao and spirulina powders; process until well combined.

3 Spoon mixture into loaf pan; press evenly along the base until approximately 1cm (½in) thick. Sprinkle with pistachios; press pistachios lightly into surface using your fingers. Refrigerate for at least 1 hour or until firm.

4 Remove from loaf pan. Trim edges; cut into 16 bars crossways.

For a less substantial snack, cut the mixture into 3cm (1¼in) squares for iron power bites (you should have 28), or roll tablespoons of the mixture for bliss balls, increasing the amount of pistachios to coat.

Popcorn snacks

serves 4

Popcorn is the perfect treat to appease your 3pm munchies

Check that the popped popcorn has cooled to room temperature before storing, because any excess moisture will cause the popcorn to stale faster.

Cheeze supreme popcorn

prep + cook time 10 minutes

Combine ¼ cup olive oil, 2 tablespoons nutritional yeast flakes, ½ teaspoon ground turmeric, 1 teaspoon onion powder and ½ teaspoon each smoked paprika and garlic powder in a large bowl. Heat 2 tablespoons olive oil in a large saucepan over medium heat. Add ½ cup popping corn, cover. Cook, shaking the pan occasionally, for 5 minutes or until the popping stops. Tip into bowl; stir to coat.

Mexican churros popcorn

prep + cook time 10 minutes

Combine ¼ cup icing (confectioners') sugar, 2 tablespoons coconut sugar, 1 tablespoon ground cinnamon, ½ teaspoon ground allspice and ½ teaspoon sea salt flakes in a large bowl. Heat 2 tablespoons olive oil in a large saucepan over medium heat. Add ½ cup popping corn, cover. Cook, shaking the pan occasionally, for 5 minutes or until the popping stops. Tip into bowl; stir to coat.

Vanilla popcorn with peanut butter caramel

prep + cook time 10 minutes

Combine ¼ cup each crunchy natural peanut butter and pure maple syrup in a small bowl. Heat 2 tablespoons olive oil in a large saucepan over medium heat. Add ½ cup popping corn and 1 teaspoon vanilla extract, cover. Cook, shaking the pan occasionally, for 5 minutes or until the popping stops. Tip into a bowl; add ½ cup finely chopped roasted salted peanuts then drizzle with peanut butter caramel to coat.

Salted caramel popcorn

prep + cook time 15 minutes

Stir 1 tablespoon rosemary leaves, 1 teaspoon sea salt flakes, ¼ cup pepitas (pumpkin seed kernels) and ¼ cup vegan margarine in a small frying pan for 3 minutes or until margarine melts and seeds are lightly toasted. Cool. Pulse 100g (3oz) vegan dark chocolate in a food processor until finely chopped. Heat 2 tablespoons vegan margarine in a saucepan over medium heat. Add ½ cup popping corn, cover. Cook, shaking the pan occasionally, for 5 minutes or until the popping stops. Add chopped chocolate and seed mixture to the pan; stir until chocolate melts and coats popcorn. Spread out onto a baking-paper-lined oven tray. Refrigerate for 5 minutes or until chocolate is set.

Choc-coated nutty dates

makes 10

10 mins
(+ standing)

do ahead

If making ahead of time, store in an airtight container in the fridge.

food swaps

Use any combination of nut butter and nuts you prefer.

100g (3oz) vegan dark chocolate (70% cocoa), chopped
10 fresh dates (200g), pitted
5 teaspoons super seed spread or nut butter
10 pecans
¼ teaspoon sea salt flakes

1 Place chocolate in a small heatproof bowl; stir over a small saucepan of simmering water until smooth (don't let the water touch base of the bowl).

2 Line an oven tray with baking paper. Cut a slit in the top of each date. Fill each date with ½ teaspoon spread and 1 pecan. Press date to enclose filling.

3 Dip dates in melted chocolate to coat; place on prepared tray. Sprinkle with salt. Stand in a cool place until chocolate is set.

makes 2½ cups

Maple & cayenne pepper trail mix

 15 mins

 food swaps

Cayenne pepper for ground cumin and pecans for cashews.

 keep it

Store trail mix in an airtight container for up to 2 weeks.

1 cup (120g) pecans
½ cup (100g) pepitas (pumpkin seed kernels)
¼ cup (40g) sunflower seeds
½ cup (35g) moist coconut flakes
¼ cup (40g) sultanas
1 tablespoon pure maple syrup
1 teaspoon sea salt flakes
¼ teaspoon cayenne pepper

1 Preheat oven to 180°C/350°F. Line an oven tray with baking paper.

2 Place pecans, pepitas, sunflower seeds, coconut flakes and sultanas in a medium bowl. Add maple syrup, salt flakes and cayenne pepper; toss to coat well. Spread mixture evenly in a single layer on tray.

3 Bake nut mixture for 10 minutes, stirring halfway through cooking or until evenly golden. Cool.

serves 8

Peanut butter & beetroot hummus

10 mins

food swaps

Use almond or macadamia spread instead of the peanut butter.

serving ideas

Serve with halved or quartered baby cucumbers.

keep it

Store hummus in the fridge for up to 3 days. The pitta bread crisps will keep in an airtight container in the pantry for up to 1 week.

3 medium beetroot (500g)
¼ cup (60ml) lemon juice
½ cup (140g) natural crunchy peanut butter
1 cup (200g) cannellini beans
1 teaspoon sea salt flakes
2 cloves garlic, peeled
¼ teaspoon ground cumin
½ cup coriander (cilantro) leaves

pitta bread crisps

2 large wholemeal lebanese bread rounds (200g)
2 tablespoons extra virgin olive oil
1 teaspoon ground cumin
1 teaspoon sumac
¼ teaspoon sea salt flakes

1 Make pitta bread crisps.

2 Wearing kitchen gloves, peel beetroot, then chop coarsely.

3 Process beetroot with remaining ingredients until smooth.

4 Serve hummus with pitta crisps.

pitta bread crisps

Preheat oven to 200°C/400°F. Using scissors, snip around edge of bread rounds, then pull apart to separate. Place crumb-side up on two large oven trays. Brush with oil; sprinkle with spices. Bake, swapping trays from top to bottom, for 4 minutes or until golden. Cool; season lightly with salt. Break into large pieces.

makes 18

Coconut & black sesame fudge

15 mins

(+ freezing)

keep it

Store in an airtight container in the freezer for up to 2 weeks. Stand at room temperature for 10 minutes to soften before serving.

1 cup (250ml) coconut cream
⅓ cup (90g) hulled tahini
2 tablespoons pure maple syrup
1 teaspoon pure vanilla extract
pinch sea salt
2 tablespoons coconut oil
1 teaspoon black sesame seeds

1 Grease a 10cm x 20cm (4in x 8in) loaf pan; line base and sides with baking paper.

2 Process coconut cream, tahini, maple syrup, vanilla, salt and coconut oil until mixture is smooth.

3 Pour into pan; sprinkle with sesame seeds. Freeze for 2 hours or until set.

4 Using an oiled sharp knife, cut into 18 pieces.

makes 24

Chocolate & almond cookies

30 mins

food swaps

You can substitute the almond oil and nuts with any other nut or nut oil. For choc-chip cookies, add 100g (3oz) chopped vegan dark chocolate to the mixture.

vegan hacks

When buying almond spread, Check the jar label to ensure the brand is vegan.

keep it

Store biscuits in an airtight container for up to 1 week.

⅓ cup (80ml) almond oil
⅔ cup (190g) almond spread (see vegan hacks)
⅔ cup (150g) firmly packed brown sugar
⅓ cup (35g) cocoa powder
¼ cup (35g) slivered almonds, chopped
1½ cups (200g) gluten-free plain (all-purpose) flour

1 Preheat oven to 160°C/325°F. Grease two oven trays and line with baking paper.

2 In a large bowl, mix oil, spread and sugar using a fork until combined. Add remaining ingredients; stir until mixture forms a soft dough.

3 Roll tablespoons of mixture into balls. Place on trays, 3cm (1¼in) apart. Press to flatten slightly with a lightly greased fork.

4 Bake for 20 minutes or until firm. Cool on trays for 10 minutes. Transfer cookies to a wire rack; cool completely.

Matcha mint raw slice

20 mins

(+ standing & refrigeration)

vegan hacks

Peppermint extract is available from health food stores. Buy peppermint extract, rather than oil or essence, or the flavour will be different.

serving ideas

Dust the top of the slice with a little extra matcha powder or top with desiccated coconut or chopped macadamias.

keep it

Store in an airtight container in the fridge for up to 6 days, or freeze for up to 2 months. Slice is best eaten within 30 minutes of removing from the freezer.

2⅓ cups (350g) raw cashews
¾ cup (100g) raw macadamias
¾ cup (60g) desiccated coconut
¾ cup (150g) coconut oil, melted
2 teaspoons light agave syrup
½ cup (125ml) coconut cream
2 teaspoons finely grated lime rind
¼ cup (60ml) lime juice
½ cup (125ml) pure maple syrup
1½ tablespoons matcha tea powder
½ teaspoon pure peppermint extract (see vegan hacks)

1 Place 2 cups of the cashews in a large bowl; cover with boiling water. Stand, covered, for 1 hour. Drain cashews, rinse under cold water; drain well.

2 Lightly grease a 20cm (8in) square cake pan; line base and sides with baking paper, extending the paper 5cm (2in) over sides.

3 Meanwhile, process remaining cashews and macadamias until crumbly. Add desiccated coconut, ¼ cup of the coconut oil and the agave syrup; process until mixture starts to come together. Press nut mixture firmly and evenly over base of pan, using a plastic spatula to form a 6mm (¼in) thick layer. Refrigerate.

4 Meanwhile, blend drained cashews and coconut cream with rind, juice, maple syrup and remaining coconut oil until as smooth as possible. Add matcha and peppermint extract; blend until combined.

5 Pour matcha mixture over base; smooth top. Cover, freeze for 3 hours or until firm. Or, refrigerate overnight.

6 Just before serving, cut matcha slice into squares.

If you have one, use a high-powered blender in step 4; this type of blender will produce a very smooth consistency.

serves 4

Rhubarb & almond galette

⧗ **30 mins**

20g (¾oz) vegan margarine, melted
275g (9oz) coarsely chopped
  rhubarb
⅓ cup (75g) firmly packed
  brown sugar
1 teaspoon finely grated orange rind
1 sheet ready-rolled vegan puff
  pastry, just thawed
2 tablespoons almond meal
10g (½oz) vegan margarine,
  melted, extra
2 teaspoons icing (confectioners')
  sugar
vanilla soy yoghurt, to serve

1 Preheat oven to 220°C/425°F. Line an oven tray with baking paper.

2 Place vegan margarine, rhubarb, sugar and rind in a medium bowl; toss until well coated.

3 Cut a 24cm (9½in) round from pastry sheet, place on lined tray; sprinkle almond meal evenly over pastry. Spread rhubarb mixture on pastry, leaving a 4cm (1½in) border; fold pastry border up and around filling. Brush edge with extra melted vegan margarine.

4 Bake galette for 20 minutes or until browned lightly. Just before serving, dust with icing sugar; serve with dollops of soy yoghurt.

TIPS

You will need 1 bunch of rhubarb for this recipe. You could use other fruit in this recipe, such as stone fruit and ripe berries.

Popcorn rocky road bark

15 mins

(+ freezing)

food swaps

Use freeze-dried strawberries or raspberries instead of the cranberries.

vegan hacks

Coconut oil has a low melting point and the syrup keeps the bark soft so eat them while still frozen.

½ cup (100g) coconut oil
½ cup (50g) cacao powder
½ cup (125ml) rice malt syrup
1 tablespoon almond butter
2 teaspoons vanilla extract
1¼ cups (25g) salted natural popcorn
1 cup (50g) flaked coconut
¾ cup (125g) dry-roasted almonds
⅓ cup (45g) dried sweetened cranberries

1 Line a 10cm x 20cm (4in x 8in) loaf pan with baking paper, extending the paper 2cm (¾in) above the edge.

2 Melt coconut oil in a medium saucepan over low heat. Remove from heat; whisk in cacao, rice malt syrup, almond butter and vanilla until cacao is dissolved and mixture is smooth.

3 Stir in three-quarters each of the popcorn, flaked coconut, almonds and cranberries. Spoon mixture into pan; spread evenly over base. Scatter with remaining popcorn, flaked coconut, almonds and cranberries; press lightly into cocoa mixture to secure.

4 Freeze bark for 15 minutes or until frozen solid.

5 Cut frozen bark into slices or chunks. Eat immediately frozen, or store in an airtight container in the freezer for up to 1 month.

Coconut & banana split pie

 20 mins

(+ standing & freezing)

 keep it

Store pie in an airtight container in the fridge for up to 3 days, or freeze at the end of step 5 for up to 2 months, then proceed with remaining steps just before serving.

1 cup (150g) raw cashews
½ cup (85g) activated buckinis (buckwheat groats)
1 cup (120g) pecans
½ cup (25g) flaked coconut
8 fresh dates (160g), pitted
2 teaspoons psyllium husks
1 teaspoon ground cinnamon
½ cup (110g) coconut oil, melted
2 ripe medium bananas (400g), mashed
½ cup (125ml) coconut cream
¼ cup (60ml) pure maple syrup
1 teaspoon pure vanilla extract
2 tablespoons black or white chia seeds
60g (2oz) vegan dark chocolate, chopped coarsely
3 medium bananas (600g), extra
1¼ cups (350g) coconut yoghurt
⅓ cup (50g) fresh cherries
½ cup (25g) flaked coconut, extra
2 tablespoons coarsely chopped pecans, extra

vegan caramel sauce
⅔ cup (160ml) coconut nectar
¼ cup (70g) cashew spread
½ teaspoon pure vanilla extract
½ teaspoon fine sea salt

1 Place cashews in a medium bowl; cover with boiling water. Stand, covered, for 1 hour. Drain cashews and rinse under cold running water; drain well.

2 Grease a 22cm (9in) pie dish.

3 Meanwhile, process buckinis, pecans, coconut, dates, psyllium, cinnamon and ¼ cup of the coconut oil until mixture resembles coarse crumbs and holds together when pressed. Using the back of a spoon, press mixture firmly over base and up side of dish to form a compact crust. Freeze while preparing filling.

4 Blend drained cashews, mashed banana, coconut cream, maple syrup and vanilla until well combined, using a high-powered blender, if available (this type of blender produces a very smooth consistency). Add remaining coconut oil; blend until smooth. Add chia seeds; pulse to combine.

5 Pour filling over base; smooth top. Freeze for 4 hours or until firm.

6 Make vegan caramel sauce.

7 Place chocolate in a small heatproof bowl over a small saucepan of gently simmering water (don't let the bowl to touch the water); stir until just melted. Set aside.

8 Slice extra bananas in half lengthways. Spoon coconut yoghurt over pie. Top with banana and cherries; drizzle with melted chocolate and caramel sauce. Sprinkle with coconut flakes and chopped pecans.

vegan caramel sauce
Blend ingredients until smooth. (Makes 1 cup.)

serves 4

Banana & tahini pudding with confetti

5 mins

serving ideas

Sprinkle confetti over fruit smoothie bowls or vegan ice-cream for added crunch.

keep it

Pudding is best made just before serving. Store the confetti in an airtight jar in the pantry for up to 2 weeks.

3 medium ripe bananas (600g), chopped coarsely
6 fresh dates (120g), pitted
⅓ cup (90g) hulled tahini
⅓ cup (80g) coconut oil, melted
2 tablespoons coconut milk
1 tablespoon pure vanilla extract
2 medium fresh figs (120g), cut into wedges

confetti
2 tablespoons activated buckwheat groats
2 tablespoons pistachios, chopped
2 tablespoons shredded coconut
2 tablespoons cacao nibs
2 teaspoons black chia seeds
2 tablespoons dried rose petals (optional)
1 tablespoon buckwheat, toasted (optional)

1 Make confetti.

2 Blend banana, dates, tahini, coconut oil, coconut milk and vanilla until as smooth as possible, using a high-powered blender if available; this type of blender will produce a very smooth consistency.

3 Spoon pudding evenly into four ¾ cup (180ml) bowls. Top with fig wedges; sprinkle with confetti.

confetti
Combine all ingredients in a small bowl. (Makes about 1 cup.)

Berry & apple crumble with 'custard'

30 mins

⅓ cup (30g) rolled oats
¼ cup (20g) flaked almonds
10g (½oz) vegan margarine
1½ tablespoons brown sugar
2 medium granny smith apples
  (300g)
1½ teaspoons vanilla bean paste
250g (8oz) strawberries, washed,
  halved

'custard'

1 medium custard apple (150g)

1 Preheat oven to 170°C/340°F. Line a small oven tray with baking paper.

2 Beat oats, almonds, vegan margarine, 1 tablespoon of the sugar and 1 teaspoon of water with an electric mixer until combined. Tip into tray, spread roughly to form clumps; bake for 10 minutes or until light golden and crunchy.

3 Meanwhile, make 'custard'.

4 Peel, core and dice apple coarsely. Place remaining sugar, ¼ cup (60ml) water, apple and vanilla in a medium saucepan over high heat; cook, stirring, for 2 minutes or until water comes to the boil. Add strawberries, stir to combine; cook for a further 8 minutes or until apple is soft and liquid is reduced by a third.

5 Divide apple mixture among four heatproof ¾ cup (180ml) ramekins or serving bowls; top each with a quarter of the oat crumble mixture. Serve each with a quarter of the 'custard'.

'custard'

Halve custard apple; discard all seeds, being careful not to discard any flesh. Process flesh in a small food processor until smooth. Cover, placing the plastic wrap directly on the surface of the puree.

TIP

Custard apples are a sub-tropical fruit with a pale green knobbly skin, a sweet creamy white flesh and brown seeds. Remove the seeds and eat the flesh when soft.

Apples & pears with walnut miso caramel

 25 mins

 vegan hacks

Check ingredients listed on the miso as some brands contain bonito (tuna) extract which is unsuitable for vegans.

 serving ideas

Serve topped with vanilla soy yoghurt.

3 small red apples (400g), halved lengthways, skin on, stems on (see tip)
3 small pears (540g), halved crossways, skin on, stems on (see tip)
2 tablespoons orange juice
2 tablespoons dark brown sugar
150g (4½oz) blackberries
125g (4oz) raspberries

walnut miso caramel

½ cup (110g) firmly packed dark brown sugar
2 tablespoons white (shiro) miso (see vegan hacks)
1 teaspoon ground cinnamon
1 cup (100g) walnuts, roasted
½ cup (125ml) fresh orange juice

1 Preheat oven to 200°C/400°F. Line two shallow-sided oven trays with baking paper.

2 Toss fruit with juice and sugar in a medium bowl; divide between trays. Roast fruit for 25 minutes, turning occasionally, or until just tender (see tip).

3 Meanwhile, make the walnut miso caramel.

4 Serve roasted fruit drizzled with caramel, topped with berries and remaining walnuts.

walnut miso caramel

Combine sugar, miso, cinnamon, half of the walnuts and juice in a medium saucepan over high heat; bring to the boil. Reduce heat; simmer, stirring occasionally, for 5 minutes or until thickened slightly.

TIP

Keep an eye on the cooking time of the apples and pears, as it will differ depending on the size and ripeness of the fruit. The fruit is done when you can insert a knife easily without resistance.

Grilled mango cheeks with lime drizzle

2 small ripe mangoes (600g)
1 tablespoon brown sugar
4 fresh kaffir lime leaves
1 tablespoon pure maple syrup
2 tablespoons lime juice
pineapple, coconut and lime sorbet,
    to serve

1 Heat a grill plate (or grill pan) over high heat. Cut cheeks from mangoes using a sharp knife. Cut each cheek into three wedges. Sprinkle each piece evenly with brown sugar.

2 Grill mango wedges, flesh-side down, for 1 minute or until just caramelised and grill lines appear.

3 Finely chop half the lime leaves; shred remaining lime leaves. Combine maple syrup, lime juice and chopped lime leaves in a small jug.

4 Spoon lime drizzle over grilled mango and sprinkle with shredded lime leaves. Serve with sorbet.

 10 mins

 food swaps

Use your favourite vegan fruit sorbet.

Melon salad with lime & mint ice

serves 4

⏳ **20 mins**

½ large pineapple (1kg)
½ medium rockmelon (850g)
1.2kg (2½lb) piece seedless
 watermelon
⅓ cup finely chopped mint
2 tablespoons icing (confectioners')
 sugar
1 tablespoon lime juice
2 cups ice cubes
small mint leaves, extra, to serve

1 Peel and thinly slice pineapple, rockmelon and watermelon. Layer fruit on serving plate or in individual bowls.

2 Blend or process mint, sugar, juice and ice cubes until ice is crushed.

3 Serve melon salad topped with lime and mint ice; sprinkle with extra mint leaves.

serves 4

Rice puddings with cinnamon & raspberries

30 mins

food swaps

Use orange rind instead of lemon rind, and nutmeg instead of cinnamon, if preferred.

serving ideas

Serve puddings with extra almond milk, if you like.

⅓ cup (65g) white medium-grain rice
2 cups (500ml) almond milk
¼ cup pure maple syrup
1 teaspoon finely grated lemon rind
2 teaspoons vanilla extract
125g (4oz) fresh raspberries, torn
½ teaspoon ground cinnamon

1 Rinse rice under cold running water until water runs clear.

2 Place almond milk, ¾ cup (180ml) water, 1 tablespoon of the maple syrup, the rind and vanilla in a small saucepan; bring to a simmer. Add rice, stirring to separate grains; bring to the boil. Reduce heat to low; cook, stirring occasionally, for 20 minutes or until rice is tender and liquid reduces and thickens.

3 Divide rice mixture among four ½-cup (125ml) shallow ovenproof dishes. Top each with a quarter of the raspberries; fold gently to mix, taking care not to break up raspberries further. Drizzle with remaining maple syrup; sprinkle with cinnamon.

4 Preheat oven grill (broiler) to high; grill for 3 minutes or until tops are golden. Serve warm.

Almond milk & mango pikelets

serves 4

 25 mins

(+ standing)

serving ideas

Serve with vegan vanilla ice-cream.

1½ cups (225g) self-raising flour
1 teaspoon baking powder
1 tablespoon golden caster (superfine) sugar
1⅓ cups (375ml) almond milk
1 tablespoon coconut oil, melted
½ teaspoon vanilla extract
¼ cup (55g) firmly packed brown sugar
2 small mangoes (600g), sliced
⅓ cup (25g) natural flaked almonds, roasted (optional) (see tip)

1 Sift flour, baking powder and caster sugar into a medium bowl. Gradually whisk in almond milk, coconut oil and vanilla until smooth. Stand for 15 minutes.

2 Heat a non-stick frying pan over medium heat. Using 2 tablespoons of batter for each pikelet, cook about four pikelets at a time for 2 minutes or until bubbles appear on the surface. Turn; cook until golden. Remove pikelets from pan; cover to keep warm. Repeat with remaining batter to make 12 pikelets in total.

3 Heat ½ cup (125ml) water and brown sugar in a medium frying pan over low heat, stirring, until dissolved. Bring to the boil. Boil for 3 minutes or until mixture thickens slightly.

4 Serve pikelets with mango, caramel sauce and almonds, if you like.

TIP

Roasting nuts brings out the flavour. Spread nuts onto an oven tray, roast in 180°C/350°F oven for around 5 to 10 minutes, or until nuts are golden brown.

Raw blueberry lemon cheesecake

 30 mins
(+ standing & freezing)

 do ahead

Store cake in an airtight container in the fridge for up to 5 days. The undecorated cake can be frozen in a container for up to 2 months.

You will need to start this recipe a day ahead.

3 cups (450g) raw cashews
1 cup (140g) macadamias
½ cup (40g) desiccated coconut
5 fresh dates (100g), pitted
½ cup (60g) pecans
¼ teaspoon salt
⅓ cup (80ml) coconut cream
½ cup (125ml) light agave syrup or ⅔ cup (160ml) pure maple syrup
1½ tablespoons finely grated lemon rind
⅓ cup (80ml) lemon juice
½ teaspoon vanilla bean paste
⅔ cup (140g) coconut oil, melted
40g (1½oz) cacao butter, melted
1½ cups (225g) frozen blueberries
125g (4oz) fresh blueberries (optional)
1 large lemon, sliced thinly (optional)

1 Place cashews in a medium bowl; cover with boiling water. Stand, covered, for 1 hour. Drain cashews, rinse under cold water; drain well.

2 Grease a 20cm (8in) round springform cake pan. Line base and side with baking paper.

3 Meanwhile, process macadamias, desiccated coconut and dates until mixture resembles coarse crumbs. Add pecans and salt; process until combined and mixture starts to stick together. Press nut mixture firmly and evenly over base of pan using a plastic spatula. Freeze until required.

4 Blend drained cashews, coconut cream, syrup, rind, juice and vanilla until as smooth as possible. Add coconut oil and cacao butter; process until well combined and very smooth.

5 Pour two-thirds of the lemon filling over base; smooth top. Scatter with ½ cup frozen blueberries; press berries lightly into filling. Freeze for 1 hour to firm up a little.

6 Meanwhile, thaw remaining frozen blueberries. Add blueberries and any juice to remaining lemon filling; blend until as smooth as possible. Spread blueberry filling over lemon filling; smooth top. Freeze cake for 4 hours or until firm.

7 Remove cake from pan; place on a plate. Decorate with fresh blueberries, and lemon slices, if you like.

 TIP

If you have one, use a high-powered blender in steps 4 and 6; this type of blender will produce a very smooth consistency. Cheesecake is best eaten within 30 minutes of removing from freezer.

Sweet drinks

serves 2

These hot chocolate flavours will comfort you all winter long

Don't miss out on your tim tam slam, with great vegan alternatives for some of your fave chocolate biscuits now readily available in most major supermarkets.

Persian chocolate

prep + cook time 15 minutes

Pit and finely chop 8 medjool dates (160g). Place ¼ cup dutch-processed cocoa and ¼ teaspoon ground cardamom in a medium deep saucepan; slowly whisk in 2½ cups almond milk until well combined. Add chopped dates; slowly bring to the boil over low heat. Using a stick blender, blend on low speed until smooth. Add 1 teaspoon vanilla bean paste and 2 teaspoons rose water; stir until combined. (Taste the mixture and adjust the taste of the rose water as brands vary.) Pour into two large mugs. Top each mug with a handful of rose-flavoured pasmak (persian fairly floss), topped with 2 tablespoons slivered pistachios, 1 tablespoon cocoa nibs and dried rose petals, if you like.

Spanish hot chocolate

prep + cook time 15 minutes

Pour 2½ cups (625ml) almond milk into a medium saucepan with 2 cinnamon sticks. Remove 2 tablespoons milk from pan; stir together with 3 teaspoons cornflour (cornstarch) in a small cup to a smooth paste. Slowly bring milk almost to the boil over low heat so the milk has time to absorb the cinnamon flavour. Add 150g (4½oz) finely chopped vegan dark chocolate, cornflour mixture and a pinch of chilli powder; whisk until chocolate melts and mixture boils and thickens slightly. Discard cinnamon sticks. Pour into two large mugs. Top with extra grated vegan dark chocolate, dust with cocoa and a pinch of ground chilli.

Salted white caramel

prep + cook time 15 minutes

Sprinkle ⅓ cup caster (superfine) sugar and ½ teaspoon crumbled salt flakes over the base of a medium heavy-based saucepan. Place pan over low-medium heat; cook without stirring until sugar dissolves and forms a golden caramel. Immediately add 20g (¾oz) coconut oil and ½ cup coconut cream; stir until caramel melts. Remove from heat; remove ¼ cup caramel mixture. Gradually stir 2 cups (500ml) almond milk and 2 teaspoons cornflour (cornstarch) into remaining caramel mixture in pan; cook, stirring, until mixture boils and thickens slightly. Pour into two large mugs. Top with a dollop of whipped coconut cream and reserved caramel. Scatter with caramel popcorn, if you like.

Spiced & spiked chocolate

prep + cook time 20 minutes

Place ½ cup water, ½ medium (240g) sliced orange, 2 whole star anise, ¼ cup firmly packed brown sugar and ⅓ cup spiced rum in a small saucepan; simmer gently over low heat until syrupy. Remove star anise and orange slices; discard. Stir in 150g (4½oz) finely chopped vegan dark chocolate until melted and smooth. Stir in 2 cups (500ml) almond milk; bring to a simmer, stirring occasionally. Pour into two large mugs. Top with a generous scoop of vegan vanilla ice-cream; dust with cocoa and sprinkle with finely grated orange rind.

Pear, maple & cashew tarts

serves
4

1 large pear (330g)
1 sheet vegan puff pastry
20g (¾oz) vegan margarine, melted
¼ cup (60ml) pure maple syrup
¼ cup (40g) cashews, halved
2 teaspoons cinnamon sugar
1 cup (280g) coconut yoghurt

1 Preheat oven to 220°C/425°F. Grease a large oven tray; line with baking paper.

2 Using a mandoline or V-slicer, slice unpeeled pear thinly lengthways.

3 Cut pastry sheet in half lengthways; place on tray. Arrange pear on pastry. Brush with vegan margarine and half the maple syrup. Top with cashews and sprinkle with half the cinnamon sugar.

4 Bake tarts for 20 minutes or until pastry is browned.

5 Combine coconut yoghurt and remaining cinnamon sugar in a bowl. Drizzle hot tarts with remaining maple syrup; serve with coconut yoghurt.

 30 mins

 vegan hacks

Cinnamon sugar is available in the spice section of the supermarket.

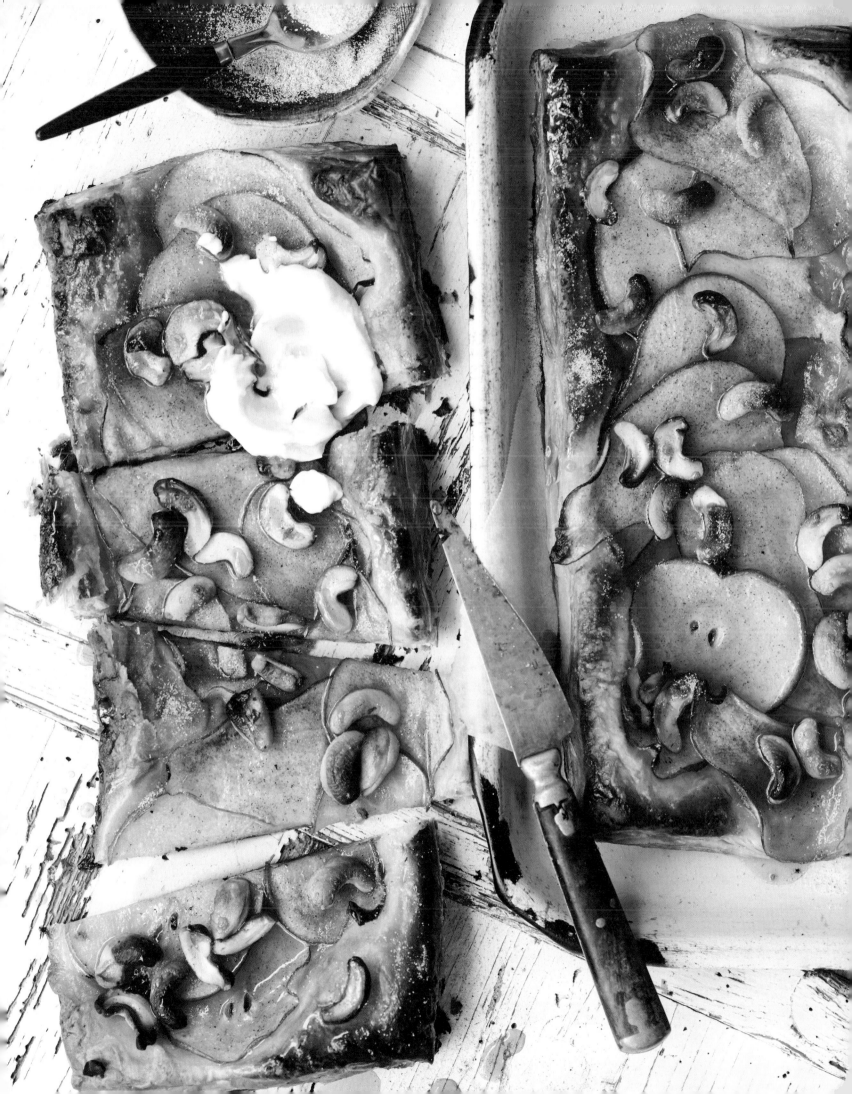

serves 4

4-Ingredient berry soft serve

 5 mins

 keep it

Store, covered, in the fridge for up to 4 days.

1½ cups (225g) frozen raspberries, plus extra to serve
¾ cup (115g) fresh blueberries, plus extra to serve
300g (9½oz) silken tofu
¼ cup (60ml) pure maple syrup

1 Blend berries, tofu and maple syrup until as smooth as possible using a high-powered blender if available; this type of blender will produce a very smooth consistency.

2 Spoon soft serve evenly into four ¾-cup (180ml) glasses. Serve immediately, topped with extra berries.

Glossary

ALLSPICE also known as pimento or jamaican pepper; so-named because it tastes like a combination of nutmeg, cumin, clove and cinnamon. Available whole or ground.

ALMONDS

flaked paper-thin slices of blanched or natural almonds.

meal also known as ground almonds; powdered to a coarse flour-like texture.

slivered small pieces cut lengthways.

BAKING POWDER a raising agent consisting mainly of two parts cream of tartar to one part bicarbonate of soda.

BASIL, THAI also known as horapa; different from holy basil and sweet basil in both look and taste, with smaller leaves and purplish stems. It has a slight aniseed taste and is one of the identifying flavours of Thai food.

BEANS

black also called turtle beans or black kidney beans; an earthy-flavoured dried bean. Used mostly in Mexican and South American cooking.

broad (fava) also called windsor and horse beans; available dried, fresh, canned and frozen. Fresh should be peeled twice (discarding both the outer long green pod and the beige-green tough inner shell); the frozen beans have had their pods removed but the beige shell still needs removal.

butter cans labelled butter beans are, in fact, cannellini beans. Confusingly butter is also another name for lima beans, sold both dried and canned; a large beige bean having a mealy texture and mild taste.

cannellini small white bean similar in appearance and flavour to other phaseolus vulgaris varieties (great northern, navy or haricot). Available dried or canned.

green also known as french or string beans (although the tough string they once had has generally been bred out of them), this long thin fresh bean is consumed in its entirety once cooked.

sprouts tender new growths of assorted beans and seeds germinated for consumption as sprouts.

BICARBONATE OF SODA (BAKING SODA) a raising agent.

BROCCOLINI a cross between broccoli and Chinese kale; long asparagus-like stems with a long loose floret, both completely edible. Resembles broccoli but is milder and sweeter in taste.

BUCKWHEAT a herb in the same plant family as rhubarb; not a cereal so it is gluten-free. Available as flour; ground (cracked) into coarse, medium or fine granules (kasha) and used similarly to polenta; or groats, the whole kernel sold roasted as a cereal product.

CACAO

butter is rich in saturated fats; about a third is stearic acid, but this acts differently to other saturated fats in that it doesn't raise cholesterol and, in fact, lowers LDL (bad) cholesterol. It is available from some health food stores and gourmet food stores.

nibs can be separated into cocoa butter and powder. Cocoa powder retains many beneficial antioxidants and is an easy way of adding cocoa into your diet without the kilojoules of chocolate.

powder is made by removing the cocoa butter using a process known as cold-pressing. It retains more of its nutrients than heat-processed cacao powder; it also has a stronger, slightly bitter, taste.

CARDAMOM a spice native to India and used extensively in its cuisine; can be purchased in pod, seed or ground form. Has a distinctive aromatic, rich flavour.

CHIA SEEDS contain protein and all the essential amino acids, as well as being fibre-rich and a wealth of vitamins, minerals and antioxidants.

CHICKPEAS (GARBANZO BEANS) an irregularly round, sandy-coloured legume. Firm texture even after cooking, a floury mouth-feel and robust nutty flavour; available canned or dried.

CHILLI

cayenne pepper a thin-fleshed, long, extremely hot dried red chilli, usually purchased ground.

flakes dried, deep-red, dehydrated chilli slices and whole seeds.

green any unripened chilli; also some particular varieties that are ripe when green, such as jalapeño, habanero, poblano or serrano.

jalapeño pronounced hah-lah-pain-yo. Fairly hot, medium-sized, plump, dark green chilli; available pickled, sold canned or bottled, and fresh, from greengrocers.

long red available both fresh and dried; a generic term used for any moderately hot, thin, long (6-8cm/2¼-3¼ inch) chilli.

powder the Asian variety is the hottest, made from dried ground thai chillies; can be used instead of fresh in the proportion of ½ teaspoon chilli powder to 1 medium chopped fresh red chilli.

small red thai (serrano) chillies, also known as "scuds"; tiny, very hot and bright red in colour.

CHOY SUM also known as pakaukeo or flowering cabbage, a member of the buk choy family; easy to identify with its long stems, light green leaves and yellow flowers. Stems and leaves are both edible, steamed or stir-fried.

CINNAMON available both in the piece (called sticks or quills) and ground into powder; one of the world's most common spices. The dried inner bark of the shoots of the Sri Lankan native cinnamon tree; much of what is sold as the real thing is in fact cassia, Chinese cinnamon, from the bark of the cassia tree. Less expensive to process than true cinnamon, it is often blended with Sri Lankan cinnamon to produce the type of "cinnamon" most commonly found in supermarkets.

COCOA POWDER also known as unsweetened cocoa; cocoa beans (cacao seeds) that have been fermented, roasted, shelled and ground into powder then cleared of most of the fat content.

dutch-processed is treated with an alkali to neutralise its acids. It has a reddish-brown colour, a mild flavour and easily dissolves in liquids.

COCONUT

cream comes from the first pressing of the coconut flesh, without the addition of water; the second pressing (less rich) is sold as coconut milk. Look for coconut cream labelled as 100% coconut, without added emulsifiers.

desiccated dried, unsweetened and finely shredded coconut flesh.

flaked dried flaked coconut flesh.

milk not the liquid found inside the fruit (coconut water), but the diluted liquid from the second pressing of the white flesh of a mature coconut (the first pressing produces coconut cream).

oil is extracted from the coconut flesh so you don't get any of the fibre, protein or carbohydrates present in the whole coconut. The best quality is virgin coconut oil, which is the oil pressed from the dried coconut flesh, and doesn't include the use of solvents or other refining processes.

shredded thin strips of dried coconut.

sugar *see Sugar*

water is the liquid from the centre of a young green coconut. It has fewer kilojoules than fruit juice, with no fat or protein. There are sugars present, but these are slowly absorbed giving coconut water a low GI.

CORIANDER (CILANTRO) also known
as pak chee or chinese parsley; a bright-green leafy herb with a pungent flavour. Both stems and roots of coriander are also used in cooking; wash well before using. Also available ground or as seeds; these should not be substituted for fresh as the tastes are completely different.

CORNFLOUR (CORNSTARCH)
available made from corn or wheat (wheaten cornflour, which contains gluten, gives a lighter texture in cakes); used as a thickening agent in cooking.

COUSCOUS a fine, grain-like cereal product made from semolina; from the countries of North Africa. A semolina flour and water dough is sieved then dehydrated to produce minuscule even-sized pellets of couscous; it is rehydrated by steaming or with the addition of a warm liquid and swells to three times its original size; eaten as a side dish or salad ingredient.

CUMIN also called zeera or comino; resembling caraway in size, cumin is the dried seed of a plant related to the parsley family. Available dried as seeds or ground, it has a spicy, almost curry-like flavour.

CURRANTS tiny, almost black raisins so-named after a grape variety that originated in Corinth, Greece.

CURRY PASTES commercially prepared curry pastes vary in strength and flavour; use whichever one you feel best suits your spice-level tolerance.

DAIKON also called white radish; an everyday fixture at the Japanese table, this long, white horseradish has a wonderful, sweet flavour. After peeling, eat it raw in salads or shredded as a garnish; also great when sliced or cubed and cooked in stir-fries and casseroles. The flesh is white but the skin can be either white or black; buy those that are firm and unwrinkled from Asian food shops.

EDAMAME (shelled soybeans) available frozen from Asian food stores and some supermarkets.

EGGPLANT also called aubergine. Ranging in size from tiny to very large and in colour from pale green to deep purple.

FENNEL a white to very pale green-white, firm, crisp, roundish vegetable about 8-12cm (3¼-4¾in) in diameter. Bulb has a slightly sweet, anise flavour but the leaves have a much stronger taste. Also the name of dried seeds having a licorice flavour.

FIVE-SPICE POWDER although the ingredients vary from country to country, five-spice is usually a fragrant mixture of ground cinnamon, cloves, star anise, sichuan pepper and fennel seeds. Used in Chinese and other Asian cooking; available from most supermarkets or Asian food shops.

FLOUR

chickpea (besan) a creamy yellow flour made from chickpeas that is very nutritious.

plain (all-purpose) a general all-purpose wheat flour.

rice very fine, almost powdery, gluten-free flour; made from ground white rice. Used in baking, as a thickener, and in some Asian noodles and desserts.

self-raising plain flour sifted with baking powder in the proportion of 1 cup flour to 2 teaspoons baking powder.

GAI LAN also called gai larn, chinese broccoli and chinese kale; green vegetable appreciated more for its stems than its coarse leaves. Can be served steamed and stir-fried, in soups and noodle dishes.

GINGER

fresh also called green or root ginger; the thick gnarled root of a tropical plant. Can be kept, peeled, covered with dry sherry in a jar and refrigerated, or frozen in an airtight container.

pickled pink or red coloured; available, packaged, from Asian food shops. Pickled paper-thin shavings of ginger in a mixture of vinegar, sugar and natural colouring; used in Japanese cooking.

HARISSA a Moroccan paste made from dried chillies, cumin, garlic, oil and caraway seeds. Available from Middle Eastern food shops and supermarkets.

HAZELNUTS also known as filberts; plump, grape-sized, rich, sweet nut having a brown skin that is removed by rubbing heated nuts together vigorously in a clean tea-towel.

meal is made by grounding the hazelnuts to a coarse flour texture for use in baking or as a thickening agent.

KAFFIR LIME LEAVES also known as bai magrood and looks like two glossy dark green leaves joined end to end, forming a rounded hourglass shape. Used fresh or dried in many South-East Asian dishes, they are used like bay leaves or curry leaves, especially in Thai cooking. Sold fresh, dried or frozen, the dried leaves are less potent so double the number if using them as a substitute for fresh; a strip of fresh lime peel may be substituted for each kaffir lime leaf.

LEMONGRASS also known as takrai, serai or serah. A tall, clumping, lemon-smelling and tasting, sharp-edged aromatic tropical grass; the white lower part of the stem is used, finely chopped, in much of the cooking of South-East Asia. Can be found, fresh, dried, powdered and frozen, in supermarkets, greengrocers and Asian food shops.

LENTILS (RED, BROWN, YELLOW)
dried pulses often identified by and named after their colour. Eaten by cultures all over the world, most famously perhaps in the dhals of India.

French-style a local cousin to the famous (and very expensive) French lentils du puy; green-blue, tiny lentils with a nutty, earthy flavour and a hardy nature that allows them to be rapidly cooked without disintegrating.

LINSEEDS (FLAXSEEDS) are slightly larger than sesame seeds and contain high levels of omega-3 fatty acids.

MACADAMIAS native to Australia; fairly large, slightly soft, buttery rich nut. Used to make oil and macadamia butter; equally good in salads or cakes and pastries; delicious eaten on their own

MAPLE SYRUP, PURE distilled from the sap of sugar maple trees. Maple-flavoured syrup or pancake syrup is not an adequate substitute for the real thing.

MISO fermented soybean paste. There are many types of miso, each with its own aroma, flavour, colour and texture; it can be kept, airtight, for up to a year in the fridge. Buy in tubs or plastic packs.

MIXED SPICE a classic spice mix containing caraway, allspice, coriander, cumin, nutmeg and ginger, although cinnamon and other spices can be added.

MUSTARD

american-style bright yellow in colour, a sweet mustard containing mustard seeds, sugar, salt, spices and garlic.

dijon pale brown, distinctively flavoured, mild french mustard.

NORI a type of dried seaweed used as a flavouring, garnish or for sushi. Sold in thin sheets, plain or toasted (yaki-nori).

NUTRITIONAL YEAST FLAKES
a seasoning used to provide a moreish cheese-like umami taste. They are a complete protein and a good source of B vitamins. Look for a brand that is fortified with B12, a vitamin required for the development of healthy blood cells and the prevention of anaemia, which is only available from fortified foods or via a supplement in a vegan diet. Available from health food stores.

OIL

coconut *see Coconut*

grapeseed comes from grape seeds; available from supermarkets.

olive made from ripened olives. Extra virgin and virgin are the first and second press, respectively, of the olives; "light" refers to taste not fat levels.

peanut pressed from ground peanuts; most commonly used oil in Asian cooking because of its high smoke point (capacity to handle high heat without burning).

sesame used as a flavouring rather than a cooking medium.

vegetable oils sourced from plant fats.

OKRA also known as bamia or lady fingers. A green, ridged, oblong pod with a furry skin. Native to Africa, this vegetable is used in Indian, Middle Eastern and South American cooking. Can be eaten on its own; as part of a casserole, curry or gumbo; used to thicken stews or gravies.

ONIONS

brown and white are interchangeable; white onions have a more pungent flesh.

green (scallions) also called, incorrectly, shallot; an immature onion picked before the bulb has formed, has a long, bright-green stalk.

red also known as spanish, red spanish or bermuda onion; a sweet-flavoured, large, purple-red onion.

OREGANO a herb, also known as wild marjoram; has a woody stalk and clumps of tiny, dark-green leaves. Has a pungent, peppery flavour.

PAPRIKA ground, dried, sweet red capsicum (bell pepper); available as sweet, hot, mild and smoked.

PARSLEY a versatile herb with a fresh, earthy flavour. There are about 30 varieties of curly parsley; the flat-leaf variety (also called continental or italian parsley) is stronger in flavour and darker in colour.

PASTRY SHEETS ready-rolled packaged sheets of frozen puff and shortcrust pastry, available from supermarkets.

PEANUTS also known as groundnut, not in fact a nut but the pod of a legume. We mainly use raw (unroasted) or unsalted roasted peanuts.

PEPITAS (PUMPKIN SEED KERNELS)
are the pale green kernels of dried pumpkin seeds; available plain or salted.

PINE NUTS not a nut but a small, cream-coloured kernel from pine cones. Toast before use to bring out their flavour.

PISTACHIOS green, delicately flavoured nuts inside hard off-white shells. Available salted or unsalted in their shells; you can also get them shelled.

POLENTA also known as cornmeal; a flour-like cereal made of ground corn (maize). Also the name of the dish made from it.

POMEGRANATE dark-red, leathery-skinned fruit about the size of an orange filled with hundreds of seeds, each wrapped in an edible lucent-crimson pulp with a unique tangy sweet-sour flavour.

QUINOA pronounced keen-wa; is cooked and eaten as a grain, but is in fact a seed. It has a delicate, slightly nutty taste and chewy texture.

flakes the grains have been rolled and flattened.

RHUBARB a plant with long, green-red stalks; becomes sweet and edible when cooked.

RICE MALT SYRUP also known as brown rice syrup or rice syrup; is made by cooking brown rice flour with enzymes to break down its starch into sugars from which the water is removed.

ROASTING/TOASTING desiccated coconut, pine nuts and sesame seeds roast more evenly if stirred over low heat in a heavy-based frying pan; their natural oils will help turn them golden. Remove from pan immediately. Nuts and dried coconut can be roasted in the oven to release their aromatic essential oils. Spread evenly onto an oven tray, roast at 180°C/350°F for about 5 minutes.

ROCKET (ARUGULA) also called rugula and rucola; peppery green leaf eaten raw in salads or used in cooking. Baby rocket leaves are smaller and less peppery.

ROLLED OATS flattened oat grain rolled into flakes and traditionally used for porridge. Instant oats are also available, but use traditional oats for baking.

SESAME SEEDS black and white are the most common of this small oval seed, however there are also red and brown varieties. The seeds are used as an ingredient and as a condiment.

SHALLOTS also called french or golden shallots or eschalots; smaller and brown-skinned.

fried can be purchased at Asian grocery stores; once opened, fried shallots will keep for months if stored in a tightly sealed glass jar.

SILVERBEET (SWISS CHARD) also called, incorrectly, spinach; has fleshy stalks and large leaves and can be prepared as for spinach.

SNOW PEAS also called mangetout; a variety of garden pea, eaten pod and all (although you may need to string them). Used in stir-fries or eaten raw in salads.

SPINACH also called english spinach and incorrectly, silver beet. Baby spinach leaves are eaten raw in salads or cooked until wilted.

STAR ANISE dried star-shaped pod with an astringent aniseed flavour; used to flavour stocks and marinades. Available whole and ground, it is an essential ingredient in chinese five-spice.

SUGAR

brown very soft, finely granulated sugar retaining molasses for its characteristic colour and flavour.

caster (superfine) finely granulated table sugar.

coconut is not made from coconuts, but from the sap of the blossoms of the coconut palm tree. The refined sap looks a little like raw or light brown sugar, and has a similar caramel flavour. It also has the same amount of kilojoules as regular table (white) sugar.

icing (confectioners') also called powdered sugar; pulverised white sugar crushed with a small amount of cornflour (cornstarch).

palm also called nam tan pip, jaggery, jawa or gula melaka; made from the sap of the sugar palm tree. Light brown to black in colour and usually sold in rock-hard cakes; use brown sugar if unavailable.

SUGAR SNAP PEAS also called honey snap peas; fresh small pea which can be eaten whole, pod and all.

SUMAC a purple-red, astringent spice ground from berries growing on shrubs that from the Mediterranean; adds a tart, lemony flavour to dips and dressings and goes well with barbecued meat. Can be found in Middle Eastern food stores.

TAHINI a rich, sesame-seed paste, used in most Middle-Eastern cuisines, especially Lebanese, in dips and sauces.

TAMARI a thick, dark soy sauce made mainly from soya beans, but without the wheat used in most standard soy sauces.

TAMARIND the tamarind tree produces clusters of hairy brown pods, each of which is filled with seeds and a viscous pulp, that are dried and pressed into the blocks of tamarind found in Asian food shops. Gives a sweet-sour, slightly astringent taste to marinades, pastes, sauces and dressings.

TEMPEH a traditional soy product originating from Indonesia. It is made by a natural culturing and controlled fermentation process that binds soybeans into a cake form.

TOFU also called bean curd; an off white, custard-like product made from the "milk" of crushed soybeans. Comes fresh as soft or firm, and processed as fried or pressed dried sheets. Fresh tofu can be refrigerated in water (changed daily) for up to 4 days.

firm made by compressing bean curd to remove most of the water. Good used in stir-fries as it can be tossed without disintegrating. Can also be flavoured, preserved in rice wine or brine.

silken not a type of tofu but reference to the manufacturing process of straining soybean liquid through silk; this denotes best quality.

TOMATO SAUCE also known as ketchup or catsup; a flavoured condiment made from tomatoes, vinegar and spices.

TOMATOES

mixed medley contains a mix of grape, baby roma, Zebrino and cherry tomatoes. Each has a distinct shape, size and flavour with colours ranging from yellow, to red and brown with stripes.

paste triple-concentrated tomato puree used to flavour soups, stews and sauces.

roma (egg) also called plum; these are smallish, oval-shaped tomatoes much used in Italian cooking or salads.

TURMERIC also called kamin; is a rhizome related to galangal and ginger. Must be grated or pounded to release its acrid aroma and pungent flavour. Known for the golden colour it imparts, fresh turmeric can be substituted with the more commonly found dried powder. When fresh turmeric is called for in a recipe, the dried powder can be substituted (proportions are 1 teaspoon of ground turmeric for every 20g of fresh turmeric).

VANILLA

bean dried, long, thin pod from a tropical golden orchid; the minuscule black seeds inside the bean are used to impart a luscious vanilla flavour in baking and desserts. A bean can be used three or four times.

extract made by extracting the flavour from the vanilla bean pod; pods are soaked, usually in alcohol, to capture the flavour.

paste made from vanilla pods and contains real seeds. Is highly concentrated – 1 teaspoon replaces a whole vanilla pod. Found in most major supermarkets in the baking section.

VINEGAR

apple cider made from fermented apples.

balsamic originally from Modena, Italy, there are now many balsamic vinegars on the market. Quality can be determined up to a point by price; use the most expensive sparingly.

rice wine made from rice wine lees, salt and alcohol.

white made from distilled grain alcohol.

wine made from white or red wine.

WOMBOK (NAPA CABBAGE) also known as Chinese cabbage or peking cabbage; elongated in shape with pale green, crinkly leaves, this is the most common cabbage in South-East Asia. Can be shredded or chopped and eaten raw or braised, steamed or stir-fried.

ZUCCHINI also called courgette; small, pale- or dark-green or yellow vegetable of the squash family.

Conversion chart

Measures

One Australian metric measuring cup holds approximately 250ml; one Australian metric tablespoon holds 20ml; one Australian metric teaspoon holds 5ml.

The difference between one country's measuring cups and another's is within a two- or three-teaspoon variance, and will not affect your cooking results. North America, New Zealand and the United Kingdom use a 15ml tablespoon.

All cup and spoon measurements are level. The most accurate way of measuring dry ingredients is to weigh them. When measuring liquids, use a clear glass or plastic jug with the metric markings.

The imperial measurements used in these recipes are approximate only. Measurements for cake pans are approximate only. Using same-shaped cake pans of a similar size should not affect the outcome of your baking. We measure the inside top of the cake pan to determine sizes.

We use large eggs with an average weight of 60g.

Dry measures

METRIC	IMPERIAL
15G	½OZ
30G	1OZ
60G	2OZ
90G	3OZ
125G	4OZ (¼LB)
155G	5OZ
185G	6OZ
220G	7OZ
250G	8OZ (½LB)
280G	9OZ
315G	10OZ
345G	11OZ
375G	12OZ (¾LB)
410G	13OZ
440G	14OZ
470G	15OZ
500G	16OZ (1LB)
750G	24OZ (1½LB)
1KG	32OZ (2LB)

Liquid measures

METRIC	IMPERIAL
30ML	1 FLUID OZ
60ML	2 FLUID OZ
100ML	3 FLUID OZ
125ML	4 FLUID OZ
150ML	5 FLUID OZ
190ML	6 FLUID OZ
250ML	8 FLUID OZ
300ML	10 FLUID OZ
500ML	16 FLUID OZ
600ML	20 FLUID OZ
1000ML (1 LITRE)	1¾ PINTS

Length measures

METRIC	IMPERIAL
3MM	⅛IN
6MM	¼IN
1CM	½IN
2CM	¾IN
2.5CM	1IN
5CM	2IN
6CM	2½IN
8CM	3IN
10CM	4IN
13CM	5IN
15CM	6IN
18CM	7IN
20CM	8IN
22CM	9IN
25CM	10IN
28CM	11IN
30CM	12IN (1FT)

Oven temperatures

The oven temperatures in this book are for conventional ovens; if you have a fan-forced oven, decrease the temperature by 10-20 degrees.

	°C (Celsius)	°F (Fahrenheit)
Very slow	120	250
Slow	150	300
Moderately slow	160	325
Moderate	180	350
Moderately hot	200	400
Hot	220	425
Very hot	240	475

A

apples
  apple pie spiced oats 37
  apples & pears with walnut miso
    caramel 215
  berry & apple crumble with 'custard'
    212
apricot & coconut balls 181
avocados
  avo rainbow salad cups 182
  avo toast with smoky crisp
    chickpeas 17
  scrambled tofu & avocado wraps 50
  super guacamole 186

B

bananas
  banana & tahini pudding with
    confetti 211
  banana with cashew butter & nutty
    crunch 178
  coconut & banana split pie 208
bánh mì not-dog 87
beans
  black beans & corn quesadillas 91
  broad bean, apple & walnut open
    sandwich 99
  chickpea pancakes with baked
    beans 95
  nourishing rainbow bean bowl 96
  polenta with rainbow chard & chilli
    beans 122
  spicy bean quesadillas 110
  spicy nachos 150
  tomato & white bean puree salad 100
beer battered potato scallops with
  minty dip 82
beetroot & pistachio crumble subs 57
berry
  4-ingredient berry soft serve 231
  berry & apple crumble with 'custard'
    212
  co-yo crunch bowl 18
bircher muesli
  make-and-go bircher 33
  pomegranate & pear 33

(*bircher muesli* continued)
  super seed 33
  tropical coconut 33
blueberry
  blueberry lemon cheesecake, raw
    224
  pie brekkie pops 38
bowls
  nourishing rainbow bean 96
  tofu poke bowl 53
breakfast
  apple pie spiced oats 37
  avo toast with smoky crisp
    chickpeas 17
  berry co-yo crunch bowl 18
  blueberry pie brekkie pops 38
  caramelised mangoes with coconut
    34
  chia crêpes with banana &
    blueberries 24
  chocolate pancakes with maple
    banana 28
  coconut quinoa pudding 45
  grilled fruit salad & coconut yoghurt
    41
  make-and-go bircher 33
  no-egg spinach & tomato omelette
    31
  orange & vanilla rawnola 42
  pea spread & fermented veg on toast
    46
  pomegranate & pear bircher 33
  power green smoothie 23
  scrambled tofu bagel 14
  soy, linseed & raspberry smoothie
    22
  spiced pecan french toast 28
  super seed bircher 33
  tropical coconut bircher 33
  warming quinoa porridge 21

C

capsicum salsa, green 107
caramel
  vegan sauce 208
  walnut miso caramel 215

cashew
  butter 178
  pear, maple & cashew tarts 228
  pesto 157
cauliflower
  cauli steaks with almonds & tahini
    126
  cauliflower & tofu red curry 161
  couscous 173
  popcorn cauliflower 133
cheesecake, raw blueberry lemon 224
chia crêpes with banana & blueberries
  24
chickpeas
  chickpea pancakes with baked
    beans 95
  spicy chickpea & yoghurt dipping
    jars 65
  sweet potato & chickpea curry 125
  sweet potatoes with chickpea
    tabbouleh 117
chilli
  chilli-lime dressing 77
  chilli peanut dressing 174
chocolate
  choc-coated nutty dates 192
  chocolate & almond cookies 200
  hot chocolate drinks 227
  iron power bars 189
  pancakes with maple banana 28
  raw choc chip cookie dough 186
coconut
  apricot & coconut balls 181
  coconut & banana split pie 208
  coconut & black sesame fudge 199
  coconut quinoa pudding 45
  coconut, tomato & lentil soup 138
  tropical coconut bircher 33
cookies, chocolate & almond 200
coriander pesto 118
corn *see also* popcorn
  black beans & corn quesadillas 91
  fritters with green papaya salad 174
  smoky sweet corn chowder 142
couscous salad, greens galore 130
crêpes, chia with banana & blueberries
  24

curries
  cauliflower & tofu red 161
  crunchy curry salad cups 92
  sweet potato & chickpea 125
  very green vegie 165

D

dates, choc-coated nutty 192
dinners
  cauli steaks with almonds & tahini 126
  cauliflower & tofu red curry 161
  cauliflower couscous 173
  coconut, tomato & lentil soup 138
  corn fritters with green papaya salad 174
  curried lentil & vegetable soup 158
  eggplant hotdog with sauerkraut 146
  fried rice 145
  gai lan & mushroom stir-fry 162
  greens galore couscous salad 130
  mushroom, spinach & walnut pasta 121
  mushroom 'steak' sandwiches 129
  pea & coconut soup 113
  polenta with rainbow chard & chilli beans 122
  popcorn cauliflower 133
  pumpkin tabbouleh 153
  salt & pepper tofu with soba noodles 170
  smoky sweet corn chowder 142
  soba noodles with chilli garlic sauce 141
  spaghetti lentil bolognese 166
  spaghetti with fresh tomatoes & seeds 133
  spaghetti with garlic & oil 133
  spaghetti with mushrooms 133
  spicy bean quesadillas 110
  spicy nachos 150
  sweet & spicy tofu noodles 114
  sweet potato & chickpea curry 125
  sweet potato & onion pizza 169
  sweet potatoes with chickpea tabbouleh 117
  tandoori tofu kebabs with mint yoghurt 149
  tofu larb with crisp rice papers 154

(dinners continued)
  vegetable spring rolls 137
  very green vegie curry 165
  zucchini & tofu noodles with coriander pesto 118
  zucchini noodles with cashew pesto 157
dressings
  chilli-lime 77
  miso peanut 66
  oregano 74
  sesame 73
  tahini 85

E

eggplant hotdog with sauerkraut 146

F

french toast, spiced pecan 28
fried rice
  chicken-like 145
  extra veg 145
  kimchi 145
  tom yum 145
fritters, corn with green papaya salad 174
fruit salad, grilled & coconut yoghurt 41
fudge, coconut & black sesame 199

G

gai lan & mushroom stir-fry 162
galette, rhubarb & almond 204
gozleme, mushroom & spinach 70
grains & greens goodness bowl 85
guacamole, super 186

H

herb salad 103
hot chocolate drinks 227
hummus, peanut butter & beetroot 196

K

kale, orange & toasted mixed seed salad 104

kimchi
  fried rice 145
  not-dog 87

L

lemon tahini dressing 182
lentils
  coconut, tomato & lentil soup 138
  curried lentil & vegetable soup 158
  spaghetti lentil bolognese 166
  tempeh chips with lentil salad 69
lunches, light
  beer battered potato scallops with minty dip 82
  beetroot & pistachio crumble subs 57
  black beans & corn quesadillas 91
  broad bean, apple & walnut open sandwich 99
  char-grilled vegie & pumpkin wrap 61
  chickpea pancakes with baked beans 95
  crunchy curry salad cups 92
  fresh samosa wraps 62
  grains & greens goodness bowl 85
  greek salad with nut fetta 74
  green mango slaw with chilli-lime dressing 77
  kale, orange & toasted mixed seed salad 104
  marinated tofu bánh mì rolls 78
  mushroom & herb salad on crunchy bread 103
  mushroom & spinach gozleme 70
  not-dogs 87
  nourishing rainbow bean bowl 96
  pea, miso & mint rice paper rolls 58
  polenta-crusted okra, asparagus & zucchini 107
  raw vegie nori rolls 81
  scrambled tofu & avocado wraps 50
  spicy chickpea & yoghurt dipping jars 65
  sprout & coriander salad 54
  tamari noodle salad jars 73
  tempeh chips with lentil salad 69
  tofu poke bowl 53
  tomato & rocket tarts 88
  tomato & white bean puree salad 100
  winter veg with miso peanut dressing 66

M

mangoes
  almond milk & mango pikelets 223
  caramelised with coconut 34
  green mango slaw with chilli-lime
    dressing 77
  grilled mango cheeks with lime
    drizzle 216
maple & cayenne pepper trail mix
  195
matcha mint raw slice 203
melon salad with lime & mint ice 219
mint
  matcha mint raw slice 203
  yoghurt 149
  yoghurt sauce 173
miso peanut dressing 66
mushroom
  gai lan & mushroom stir-fry 162
  mushroom & herb salad on crunchy
    bread 103
  mushroom & spinach gozleme 70
  mushroom, spinach & walnut pasta
    121
  mushroom 'steak' sandwiches 129
  spaghetti with mushrooms 133

N

nachos
  nacho not-dog 87
  spicy 150
noodles
  salt & pepper tofu with soba noodles
    170
  soba noodles with chilli garlic sauce
    141
  sweet & spicy tofu 114
  tamari noodle salad jars 73
  zucchini & tofu noodles with
    coriander pesto 118
  zucchini, with cashew pesto 157
not-dogs 87

O

oats see also bircher muesli
  apple pie spiced 37
  orange & vanilla rawnola 42
omelette, no-egg spinach & tomato 31

orange & vanilla rawnola 42
oregano dressing 74

P

pancakes
  almond milk & mango pikelets 223
  batter 28
  chia crêpes with banana &
    blueberries 24
  chickpea, with baked beans 95
  chocolate with maple banana 28
pasta see also spaghetti
  mushroom, spinach & walnut 121
peanut butter & beetroot hummus
  196
pears
  pear, maple & cashew tarts 228
  pears & apples with walnut miso
    caramel 215
peas
  pea & coconut soup 113
  pea, miso & mint rice paper rolls 58
  pea spread & fermented veg on toast
    46
pesto
  cashew 157
  coriander 118
pitta bread crisps 196
pizza, sweet potato & onion 169
poke bowl, tofu 53
polenta
  polenta-crusted okra, asparagus &
    zucchini 107
  polenta with rainbow chard & chilli
    beans 122
pomegranate & pear bircher 33
popcorn 191
  cheeze supreme 191
  mexican churros 191
  popcorn rocky road bark 207
  salted caramel 191
  vanilla, with peanut butter caramel
    191
pops, blueberry pie brekkie 38
porridge
  apple pie spiced oats 37
  warming quinoa 21
potato scallops, beer battered with
  minty dip 82
power green smoothie 23

pumpkin
  char-grilled vegie & pumpkin wrap
    61
  pumpkin tabbouleh 153

Q

quesadillas
  black beans & corn 91
  spicy bean 110
quinoa
  coconut quinoa pudding 45
  warming quinoa porridge 21

R

reuben not-dog 87
rhubarb & almond galette 204
rice see also fried rice
  crisp rice papers 154
  rice paper rolls, pea, miso & mint 58
  rice puddings with cinnamon &
    raspberries 220
rolls
  eggplant hotdog with sauerkraut
    146
  marinated tofu bánh mì 78
  not-dogs 87
  raw vegie nori 81

S

salads
  avo rainbow salad cups 182
  crunchy curry salad cups 92
  greek, with nut fetta 74
  green mango slaw with chilli-lime
    dressing 77
  greens galore couscous 130
  herb 103
  kale, orange & toasted mixed seed
    104
  pumpkin tabbouleh 153
  sprout & coriander 54
  tamari noodle salad jars 73
  tomato & white bean puree 100
salsa, green capsicum 107
samosa wraps, fresh 62
sandwiches
  broad bean, apple & walnut open 99
  mushroom 'steak' 129

seeds
  kale, orange & toasted mixed seed salad 104
  super seed bircher 33
sesame dressing 73
slaw, green mango with chilli-lime dressing 77
smoothies
  power green 23
  soy, linseed & raspberry 22
snacks
  apricot & coconut balls 181
  avo rainbow salad cups 182
  chocolate iron power bars 189
  maple & cayenne pepper trail mix 195
  peanut butter & beetroot hummus 196
  pitta bread crisps 196
  popcorn 191
  super guacamole 186
soba noodles
  salt & pepper tofu with soba noodles 170
  with chilli garlic sauce 141
soups
  coconut, tomato & lentil 138
  curried lentil & vegetable 158
  pea & coconut 113
  smoky sweet corn chowder 142
soy, linseed & raspberry smoothie 22
spaghetti
  spaghetti lentil bolognese 166
  with fresh tomatoes & seeds 133
  with garlic & oil 133
  with mushrooms 133
spiced pecan french toast 28
spinach & tomato omelette, no-egg 31
spring rolls, vegetable 137
sprout & coriander salad 54
stir-fry, gai lan & mushroom 162
sweet potatoes
  sweet potato & chickpea curry 125
  sweet potato & onion pizza 169
  with chickpea tabbouleh 117
sweets
  4-ingredient berry soft serve 231
  almond milk & mango pikelets 223
  apples & pears with walnut miso caramel 215
  banana & tahini pudding with confetti 211

(*sweets* continued)
  banana with cashew butter & nutty crunch 178
  berry & apple crumble with 'custard' 212
  choc-coated nutty dates 192
  chocolate & almond cookies 200
  chocolate iron power bars 189
  coconut & banana split pie 208
  coconut & black sesame fudge 199
  grilled mango cheeks with lime drizzle 216
  matcha mint raw slice 203
  melon salad with lime & mint ice 219
  pear, maple & cashew tarts 228
  popcorn rocky road bark 207
  raw blueberry lemon cheesecake 224
  raw choc chip cookie dough 186
  rhubarb & almond galette 204
  rice puddings with cinnamon & raspberries 220

T

tabbouleh, pumpkin 153
tahini
  banana & tahini pudding with confetti 211
  dressing 85
tamari noodle salad jars 73
tandoori tofu kebabs with mint yoghurt 149
tarts, tomato & rocket 88
tempeh chips with lentil salad 69
tofu
  cauliflower & tofu red curry 161
  larb with crisp rice papers 154
  marinated tofu bánh mì rolls 78
  no-egg spinach & tomato omelette 31
  salt & pepper, with soba noodles 170
  scrambled tofu & avocado wraps 50
  scrambled tofu bagel 14
  sweet & spicy tofu noodles 114
  tandoori tofu kebabs with mint yoghurt 149
  tofu poke bowl 53
  zucchini & tofu noodles with coriander pesto 118
tom yum fried rice 145

tomato
  coconut, tomato & lentil soup 138
  spaghetti with fresh tomatoes & seeds 133
  tomato & rocket tarts 88
  tomato & white bean puree salad 100
trail mix, maple & cayenne pepper 195

V

vegies
  char-grilled vegie & pumpkin wrap 61
  curried lentil & vegetable soup 158
  extra veg fried rice 145
  raw vegie nori rolls 81
  vegetable spring rolls 137
  very green vegie curry 165
  winter veg with miso peanut dressing 66

W

wraps
  char-grilled vegie & pumpkin 61
  fresh samosa 62
  scrambled tofu & avocado 50

Z

zucchini
  noodles with cashew pesto 157
  polenta-crusted okra, asparagus & zucchini 107
  zucchini & tofu noodles with coriander pesto 118